LIVES

OF THE

CHIEF FATHERS OF NEW ENGLAND.

The Lord our God be with us, as he was with our fathers; let him not leave us, nor forsake us

1 KINGS 8: 57.

VOL. I.

THE LIFE

OF

JOHN COTTON.

BY A. W. M'CLURE.

LIBRARY EDITION, 100 COPIES.

BOSTON:
1870.

GENERAL INTRODUCTION.

Veneration for departed worth is a sentiment so natural and proper, that he who is incapable of feeling it, must be regarded as hopelessly ungenerous and ignoble. The remembrance of the just is a blessing to them that cherish it. Such memories awaken a pure ambition; and lead to the virtuous resolve to emulate, to equal, to exceed the patterns we admire. The contemplation of exemplary goodness gives life to magnanimous thoughts, and beneficent purposes. It is wise to multiply these lessons, and to surround ourselves with these incentives of excellence. The Egyptian graced his habitation with the embalmed persons of his ancestry, hoping that thus their merits might linger in the abode of their descendants. The Grecian multiplied the statues of those who had been distinguished for public or private virtues, believing that the mute eloquence of the sculptured stone would not plead in vain for that respect which ends in imitation. So too let us adorn our dwellings with the memorials of the great and good. Let them be embalmed with the odorous spices of grateful remembrance. Let the very walls of our houses, garnished with their portraitures and the pictured story of their deeds, summon us to a righteous emulation. The trophies of Miltiades would not suffer Themistocles to sleep.

As for us, whose homes are on the soil of New England, we need not go far from our birthplace, to find the most illustrious examples to be studied and copied. Since the days of the apostles, there have been no worthier patterns of Christian character and primitive piety than the Puritans, to whom we are indebted for all that gives our people any superiority in any respect over other nations of the earth. Not that we are to practice an indiscriminate and idolatrous veneration. "There are no errors which are so likely to be drawn into precedent, and therefore none which it is so necessary to expose, as the errors of persons who have a just title to the gratitude and admiration of posterity. In politics, as in religion, there are devotees who show their reverence for a departed saint, by converting his tomb into a sanctuary for crime." But though the Puritans had their faults and failings, what sort of moral appetite must that be which fastens upon and devours these unsavory scraps, and neglects all that is pure and wholesome in their character? If there be any sore spot in their example, these flesh-flies detect it with unerring instinct, and dart upon it with a ravenous delight. He who can see nothing in the sun but its spots must be worse than blind; for while his eye gazes with morbid intensity on darkness, he has no vision for that which is bright and fair.

Luther has said that "evil comes of good:" which remark accords with the Rabbinical proverb, "Vinegar is the son of wine." And we find that even some of the descendants of the Puritans have proved so degenerate as, with filial impiety, to blacken and revile the memory of their sires. Foul and unnatural deed! How doth it react to the degradation and infamy of its base perpetrators! "There is no readier way," says Tillotson, "for a man to bring his own worth into question, than by endeavoring to detract from the worth of other men." And this is especially the case when the slanderer is vilifying his own progenitors. What can be more odious than to see the child defacing and polluting the sepulchre of his fathers? The only disgrace he can fix upon them, is that of having generated a monster so contemptible as himself. Such recreant and apostate natures usually exceed all others in the avidity and malignity with which they traduce the sainted dead. They do this for the reason Dryden gives, and he must have known as being one himself,

> "For renegadoes, who ne'er turn by halves,
> Are bound in conscience to be double knaves."

The mists which obscure the sun are exhaled by his own fervent beams. Envy and detraction are the shadows which ever follow shining merit. The calumniators of the Puritans serve as the shades in the picture, which render the lights more distinct and vivid. The fair fame of the Puritans shines the more luminous, when contrasted with the dark dispositions of their slanderers.

It is but justice to the pious dead to vindicate their good name, which, as Cicero says, is the appropriate possession of the departed. And justice to ourselves

1*

requires, that we should preserve untarnished the reputation of our fathers, so that we may feel its full influence to quicken our own virtues, and to stimulate them to greater activity and fruitfulness. Certain it is, that they will be the most likely to partake of the excellencies of the Puritans, who most deeply revere them.

In different ages there have arisen men, too great or too good for the times in which they lived :—men, like Israel's martyred prophets, of whom the world was not worthy. They have strode so far in advance of their cotemporaries, that as Coleridge said of Milton, they dwarfed themselves in the distance. Bitter scorn and bitterer wrath was their portion while they lived.

And after they are gone, other generations sweep by, till the same venerable worthies are again almost lost from view in the dim perspective of the past. Then are their names again decried, because they stopped where they did. The most distinguished of living British essayists has said with a just severity;—"It is too much that the benefactors of mankind, after having been reviled by the dunces of their own generation for going too far, are to be reviled by the dunces of the next generation for not going far enough."

The world shows its unworthiness of these good men, either by forgetting their virtues as soon as possible: or else by remembering their names only to traduce them. Thus thanklessly and harshly has it dealt with our pilgrim fathers. But, blessed be the Lord! there are not wanting those, who, like "Old

Mortality" among the graves of the Covenanters, with chisel in hand, revisit the resting-place of our Puritan sires, raising up the fallen monuments; removing the encroaching mosses; and, with pious care, retouching the fading inscriptions which the ceaseless stream of time is wearing away.

Such a pleasing task of filial piety and reverent love is before us in the present undertaking. Nor doubt we, that the work is well pleasing unto God, who is himself, in his providence, the Vindicator of their wisdom and zeal; and whose Word has taught us, that the memory of the just is blessed, and that the righteous must be had in everlasting remembrance.

These considerations have induced the Publishing Committee of the Massachusetts Sabbath School Society to prepare a series of biographical sketches of some of the distinguished men, who were God's instruments in making this country what it is. These volumes will collect, and present in one view, every thing which relates to them that can be recovered from scattered confusion and from oblivion. It is intended that this exhibition shall bring out the characters, actions, sufferings and principles of these remarkable men, in such form as may interest and profit the general reader, and not be unuseful to such as may be studious of the early history of our country.

The Committee have observed with pain, that there is, in some quarters, a disposition to subject the memory of the Puritans to what is sometimes significantly called "cavalier treatment." The best defence which can be made of these worthies is to show them as they were. Could such an exhibition be made to the life, it is certain that it would have the same dispersing effect upon their detractors, as the appearance of Cromwell's unconquered "Ironsides" had upon the runaways of Naseby, of Preston, and of Worcester.

It is hoped that these volumes will not only find a place in all our Sabbath school libraries, but may obtain a general circulation among the young men and young women of our land. It is believed that the contemplations of these noble examples will be found among the best means of strengthening the minds, enriching the memories, and settling the principles, of the young. The moral beauty of the character of the Puritans consist chiefly in this,—*they were men of principle.* This made them deliberate in resolving, and inflexible in performing. The "noble grace of decision" shone conspicuously in their lives; they were decided for truth, for conscience, for God. It was a rich gift of the Holy Ghost, and enabled them for a work in which all other adventurers must have failed.

May God bless this undertaking, so that it may help to revive in power and purity the remnants of the piety and spirit of the pilgrims which yet linger among us. May it help to increase the multitudes which, like the Puritans of old, have gone up, through much tribulation, from the footstool to the throne!

PREFACE.

The difficulty of preparing a work of this nature can only be conceived of by one who has tried it. The mere collecting of the scattered materials, dispersed in the obscurest corners, as they usually are, is a great labor. It is a greater toil to arrange them in due order, when once they are collected. The settling of doubtful and contradictory statements is often a tedious and perplexing business. And then comes the writing, which the author must accomplish as he can. The only merit which this little book can claim, is laborious accuracy bestowed upon a worthy subject. For its faults in other respects, there can hardly be any remedy. For, to apply here a rhyme of President Oakes,

> "They that can *Cotton's* goodness well display,
> Must be as good as he:—but who are they?"

In prosecuting the design of the Publishing Committee of the Massachusetts Sabbath School Society, it is evident that the distinctive principles of the Puritans must come under review. In order that these might be more completely presented, they are discussed somewhat fully in a few chapters devoted to that object. Accordingly, in this volume, will be found a chapter occupied with an account of the nature and origin of Puritanism, in which our fathers are vindicated from the charge of schism and sinful division of the Church. Another chapter delineates the main features of the Congregational Church government. Another still, exhibits the merits of Congregationalism.

May God grant wisdom to all who may take part in this attempt to revive the memory of the patriarchs of our land; and give to the readers grace to profit by their holy example.

"A *life* may find him who a *sermon* flies."

LIFE OF JOHN COTTON.

CHAPTER I.

His parentage. Residence at the University. Conversion.

THE man whose life and principles will now be represented, from the vast influence he exercised in his own time, and, consequently, upon all following times, has been fitly called the Patriarch of New England. Boston, especially, is indebted to him for much more than its name. He found it but little better than a woody wilderness; and he left it a flourishing town, a sort of Jerusalem of the West.

John Cotton was a native of Derby, on the river Derwent, in England. He was born on the fourth of December, in the year 1585. He was descended of 'gentle blood.' His parents were persons in easy circumstances, and able to provide him with the necessaries for a good education. The father, Roland Cotton, a lawyer by profession, was distinguished, as well as the mother, by a solid and fervid piety. The child, thus brought forth and brought up, did no discredit to his training. His youth, unstained by follies, gave no occasion for reproach in after years. It is pleasing to consider a person, who, from the cradle to the grave, lived a long life without spot or blame, other than what arose from the mistakes of those around him, or those errors of his own which serve to associate him with weak humanity, but not with its vices or its crimes. It is true, that, at certain times, amid the tempests of passion and prejudice, much mire and dirt was cast upon his character, but none of it would adhere. It all fell off again, and left his reputation unsullied as ever.

He was admitted to Trinity College, Cambridge, at the early age of thirteen. His father who had never had many clients before, from that time had them in abundance. The son, who had, in consequence, a very liberal maintenance, and who also had a watchful eye to discern the ways of divine providence, was thereby led to say :—"God kept me at the university!"

At this ancient seminary, the nursing mother of so many eminent Puritan ministers, he spent fifteen studious years, till he became learned in all the wisdom of that age of erudite scholars and deep divines. He was prevented from obtaining a fellowship in his college, only by reason of embarrassments growing out of the construction of expensive buildings for its use.

He was then chosen a fellow of Emmanuel College, after a severe examination, which he triumphantly sustained. He was examined with special rigor in the Hebrew language. He was tested more particularly upon the latter part of the third chapter of Isaiah, which consists of an inventory of the fineries of the haughty daughters of Zion, such as might well astonish a modern Parisian milliner. This passage, which contains more unusual and perplexing terms than any other in the Old Testament, occasioned no trouble to our ardent scholar, who was able to converse in that tongue. Hebrew literature was much cultivated among the Puritan divines, who gave especial attention to those three languages in which it was stated on the cross, that Jesus of Nazareth was King of the Jews. And yet the famed Erasmus, though reputed in his day to be "the most Greek among the Grecians, and the most Latin among the Latins," and though so used to discourse in the latter language as to forget his mother tongue, gave up the attempt to acquire the Hebrew in utter discouragement. This study, in which Luther so much delighted, found many expert proficients among the spiritual fathers of New England. Nearly all the first ministers of Massachusetts cultivated it: and some very singular anecdotes are preserved to illustrate their familiarity with that language, which, as John Eliot said, "it pleased our Lord Jesus Christ to make use of when he spake from heaven unto Paul." Some of the laymen bestowed great attention upon it. Thus Governor Bradford, who had thoroughly mastered some four or five other languages, studied the Hebrew most of all; "because," as he elegantly said, "he would see with his own eyes the ancient oracles of God in their native beauty!"

In the same distinguished College where he gained his fellowship, Mr. Cotton afterwards became Head Lecturer; then Dean, an officer charged to attend to the deportment and discipline of the students; and Catechist, an employment of chief note in the old conventual schools. He was also Tutor to numerous scholars, by whom he was held in the highest estimation as a teacher.

While occupied thus usefully, he was much honored and admired for the strength and readiness of his mind, and for the vast extent of his reading. The sermons, which he occasionally preached in the University, were pompous harangues, stuffed with a huge mass of learning and soaring conceits, according to the taste of the "vain wits" of that seat of science. These ostentatious displays made him very popular with that class of men, who delighted in such parades of learned lore, as much as they distasted the plain preaching of the humbling doctrines of the cross. Cotton was then one of their own sort, being himself of that lamentably numerous class who undertake to preach the gospel of Christ without having personally felt its life and power in the heart.

He first distinguished himself by a funeral discourse for Dr. Some, Master of Peter House, in which he flourished away with so much artificial originality, affected eloquence and "oratorious beauty," that he came to be regarded as the Xenophon of the University, and the special favorite of the muses. Some time after, he delivered a University sermon in St. Mary's Church, which gained the high applause of the academical pedants, who looked only for a grand exhibition of what the preacher could do to show off himself, rather than for a presentation of "Christ crucified, unto the Jews a stumbling block, and unto the Greeks foolishness; but unto them which are called, both Jews and Greeks,

Christ the power of God, and the wisdom of God."

But the Lord had other employment for this "chosen vessel." He who had dwelt so long among those halls of science as one of her most assiduous devotees, began at last to feel the higher claims of religion.

In those days there was at Cambridge an eminent and godly divine, Rev. William Perkins, whose name was long precious among our fathers, one of whom made this epigram upon him, in allusion to a certain natural defect;

"Though nature thee of thy *right* hand bereft,
Right well thou writest with thy hand that's *left*."

This good and able man was sound in the faith, and deep in the experience of the great doctrines of the gospel. His ministrations, so searching to the heart and so rousing to the conscience, were blessed to the conversion of many who became some of the brightest lights of their age. Among others, Mr. Cotton was much wrought upon by his faithful exhibition of the truth. But the young and aspiring scholar, fearing to become engaged in the pursuit of personal religion, lest it should hinder him in the studies he was ambitiously following, suppressed, so far as he could, the motions and stirrings of his mind. In the pride of intellect, and the lust of literary distinction, he resisted the strivings of the Holy Spirit. For a while, he succeeded in stifling the still small voice of conviction, till one day walking in the fields, he heard the bell tolling the death-knell of the devout Mr. Perkins. At this, Mr. Cotton secretly rejoiced; and began to congratulate himself, that he should no more be troubled by him, who had, as he said, "laid siege to and beleaguered his heart."

But this selfish satisfaction at such a riddance soon became a cause of great spiritual distress. It dwelt constantly upon his mind as an aggravated sin, that he had thus exulted at the prospect of being freed, at such a price, from divine incitements and restraints. God made it "an effectual means of convincing and humbling him in the sight and sense of the natural enmity that is in man's nature against God."

In this state of mind, he heard a sermon from Dr. Sibbs, a man of great note among the Puritans in the time of the first James. This sermon was upon the nature and necessity of regeneration. It first showed the state of the unregenerate, and the misery of those who have no righteousness but that of the moral virtues. Under this discourse, Mr. Cotton felt all his false hopes and self-righteous confidences failing him. He found the truth of what the Bible taught him, that he was a sinner in the sight of God,—that he was wholly and helplessly depraved, and utterly lost beyond the power of recovering himself. For near three years, he was fainting under the burden of desponding thoughts, feeling that he had willfully withstood the means of grace and the offers of mercy which God had extended to him. At length the barbed arrow, which so long had rankled in his heart, was plucked away. Through the same wound from which the bloody drops of contrition had flowed, the healing grace of Jesus was infused. This comfort appears to have been ministered to his soul under the preaching of the same worthy Dr. Sibbs; between whom and the happy convert there ever after subsisted "a singular and constant love," as between a spiritual father and his son in the faith.

The conversion of Mr. Cotton was of that primitive, orthodox stamp, which has always produced the best sort of Christians. There is reason to suspect that many who are in the habit of speaking of such a change in terms of levity and unbelief, would inwardly rejoice if they could be assured of undergoing the same moral renovation before they shall be summoned to the bar of God. There is something in such an experience which commends itself even to the conscience of the scoffer and profane. In the case of Mr. Cotton it was no rash and reasonless excitement: but the result of years of anxious inquiry and mental conflict. It occurred when he was at the maturity of his powers and in their highest state of discipline and development. It was a solid work, on a firm foundation, by the Almighty hand: and therefore was it a lasting monument of grace. The subject of it, at the time, was not far from twenty-seven years of age.

Ere long he was called once more to fill the old stone pulpit of St. Mary's venerable church. A numerous auditory of the University men, attracted by his high reputation, thronged the place. These were hearers, who, as the excellent John Norton said of them, and he knew them well, "prefer the Muses before Moses, and taste Plato more than Paul, and relish the Orator of Athens far above the Preacher of the Cross." They were confidently expecting to be regaled with the heaped up quotations, the philosophical abstractions, the scholastic subtleties, and rhetorical ornaments, by which the preachers on those occasions were wont to hold up to admiration, not their Master, but themselves. When Mr. Cotton arose, the hum of approbation, which used to greet a popular speaker, resounded through the temple. But their expectation was destined to be disappointed. The discourse was upon the subject of *repentance*, and was enunciated from a heart which had freshly felt the power of the theme. It was a plain, pungent, practical address, directly aimed at the conscience of the hearers. The countenances of his audience betrayed their discontent; in token of which, they pulled down their shovel-caps over their faces, and listened in sullen mood.

The poor preacher, discouraged with this cold reception of his zealous endeavors for their good, retired to his chambers with some sad thoughts of heart. He had not been long alone, when Dr. John Preston, then a fellow of Queen's College, and of great esteem in the University, knocked at his door. This person, like so many others, had repaired to the sermon, with his ears itching to hear a splendid literary performance. For a while, he manifested his vexation in every way he could: but ere the close, he was "cut to the heart" by the sword of the Spirit. Making an errand of borrowing a book, he called on Mr. Cotton, with whom he had not been acquainted. His wounded soul could not keep silence; and he sought those spiritual succors which God blessed to the peace of his mind. This man too became a powerful preacher of the gospel, and a mighty man of renown among the Calvinistic doctors of that age of giant minds. This notable seal of his ministry consoled Mr. Cotton for the manner in which his first evangelical sermon was received by the many. He never regretted that he had cast his ostentatious ways aside, and had sought only to approve himself unto God. Some of the more religious divines prayed him to "persevere in that good way of preaching," which, by the grace of God, he effectually did. How true is the remark of the excellent Thomas Fuller, "It is easier and better for us to please one God, than many men, with our sermons." Between Mr. Cotton and Dr. Preston there was formed one of those most profitable Christian friendships, which must outlast earth and heaven. There are no good men, but others are the better for them.

CHAPTER II.

Settlement at Boston in Old England. Obstacles to Settlement. Spiritual Conflicts. Arminian Controversy. Marriage. Non-Conformity.

When Mr. Cotton was about twenty-eight years of age, he was invited by the people of Boston, in Lincolnshire, to settle in the ministry among them. *Old* Boston, whose chief honor now is, that she imparted her name to her cisatlantic daughter, was indebted for it to Botolph, an ancient Saxon saint; the name Botolph's town, having been, in time, contracted to its present form. In that place, Mr. Cotton labored many years in the pastoral office, exerting a wonderful influence upon the character of the people. We read in Burke's famous speech made long afterwards on American affairs, the odd quotation from an old song;—

Solid men of Boston, make no long orations,
Solid men of Boston, drink no strong potations.

I am ready to believe that this character for solidity, for brevity of speech, and for observing the "holy dictate of spare temperance," may be owing to the labors of this man of God, leaving their impress upon the descendants of his parishioners there, as I doubt not they have done here.

Mr. Cotton's settlement was not without some difficulty. The church-warden, with the better sort of people, desired that he should be their pastor. But the mayor, with the looser class, had procured from Cambridge another candidate more to their minds. When the election came to be held under the charter, the votes were found to be equally divided. The mayor, having the casting vote, by some mistake gave it in favor of Mr. Cotton. The civic dignitary, mortified at his error, requested that the vote might be taken again. His request was complied with, and resulted as before, in an equal division. And now, strange to tell, the mayor made the same mistake, and again gave his casting vote in Mr. Cotton's favor. In great vexation, the blundering magistrate insisted upon trying the vote for the third time; but the people refused their consent. Thus the choice fell upon Mr. Cotton, through the unintended act of his most strenuous opposer.

This obstruction being removed, there came another in the way. Dr. Barlow, the diocesan, understanding that the successful candidate was infected with Puritanism, tried to discourage his settlement. The prelate's only objection was, that Mr. Cotton was too young a man to be set over such a numerous and factious people. The young man had so modest an opinion of himself, that he was satisfied with the objection, and proposed to go back to the University. But some of his supporters, understanding, as good Mr. Norton tells us, "that one Simon Bibby was to be spoken with, who was near to the bishop, they presently *charmed* him; and so the business proceeded without further trouble, and Mr. Cotton was admitted into the place after their manner in those days." It looks suspicious in this case, that the charmers operated upon the said Simon Bibby, by means of unlawful spells, perchance mingling the potency of *simony* and *bibification.* But whatever the nature of their enchantments may have been, Mr. Cotton cannot be charged with any knowledge of their proceedings.

About this time he was deeply exercised with spiritual troubles, even as his Master was subjected to temptation at the beginning of *his* public ministry. There is much truth in Luther's saying, "that three things make a divine; meditation, supplication, and temptation." It is probable that few ministers have ever been extensively useful in the Church of God, without first passing through severe conflicts of mind against doubts, and fears, and unbelief; before coming to the settled enjoyment of the consolations and supports of the gospel. Taught both by sterner and by sweeter experience, they learn how to guide others through similar spiritual difficulties. It is thus that they become "able to comfort them which are in any trouble, by the comfort wherewith they themselves are comforted of God."

Engrossed as he was in these severe mental trials, Mr. Cotton paid no heed to the parties and factions which disturbed the town. This sort of impartiality conciliated the good will of the people, when they saw that the salvation of his own soul was far more upon his thoughts, than the contentions and disputes around him.

At that time, there was a Mr. Baron in the place, a man very skillful in his calling, as a physician, but who chiefly devoted his studies to the defence of Arminianism, which he maintained on all occasions, with much acuteness and ability. To his constant conversation, Mr. Cotton silently listened, till he "had learned, at length, where all the great strength of the doctor lay." Having mastered all Mr. Baron's scruples and objections, and, avoiding all those expressions and phrases of others, which afforded that gentleman any advantage in debate, Mr. Cotton began publicly to preach the doctrine of God's eternal election; the effectual calling of the sinner by irresistible grace; and the certain perseverance of saints, so that they shall not fall from a state of grace, either totally or finally. The result was, that the adverse disputant desisted from all further debate; Arminianism died quite away, without struggle or convulsion, "and all matters of religion were carried on calmly and peaceably."

When he had resided at his parish about half a year, he visited Cambridge, to take his degree of Bachelor of Divinity. On this occasion, he added largely to his reputation, by a much admired sermon to the clergy, from the text; "Ye are the salt of the earth; but if the salt have lost his savor, wherewith shall it be salted?" He also distinguished himself by his skill in a public disputation, held in the schools for the purpose of proving himself qualified for his degree in divinity. He appeared to high advantage, though matched against a very keen debater, a Dr. Chappell; afterwards Provost of Trinity College, in Dublin, and a strenuous advocate of Pelagian sentiments. After gathering these University laurels, Mr. Cotton returned to his parochial charge, where he enjoyed the high esteem of his flock. It is a remark of one of his fellow-laborers, "So God disposeth of the hearts of hearers, as that generally they are all open and loving to their preachers in their first times; trials are often reserved until afterwards. Epiphanius calleth the first year of Christ's ministry, the acceptable year.—*Young* Peter girdeth himself, and walks whither he will; but *old* Peter is girded by another, and carried whither he would not."

Being comfortably settled in his church, he married Elizabeth Horrocks, "an eminently virtuous gentlewoman." The day of their union, was ever memorable to him, upon another account; for it was then, that he first received a comfortable assurance of God's love to his soul. The promises of grace and life, were sealed upon his heart by the Holy Spirit; and this comfort continued with him, in some happy measure, through the residue of his days. He would often say of the day of his espousals, "God made it a day of double marriage to me!" for it was then that he obtained the blessed evidence of the marriage-union of his soul with Christ.

His worthy companion was of great assistance to him in his ministry, in many respects; but especially in this, that she greatly promoted his usefulness among those of her own sex. The female members of the congregation, taking notice of her uncommon discretion and piety, would freely impart to her the state of their minds upon the subject of religion, acquainting her with their difficulties, and the points on which they stood in need of special counsel and instruction. The information she imparted to her husband, enabled him to adapt his public teaching to the wants of his hearers, and to render it far more conducive to their spiritual good. If experience can prove any thing, it has abundantly proved that the judicious marriage of a clergyman greatly enhances his usefulness, and his estimation among his flock. It not only places him as "a family man," in close sympathy with the families of his flock, but it puts him in unexceptionable communication with the female portion of his charge. He thus obtains a sufficiently confidential knowledge of the condition of their minds, and also the opportunity of meeting their wants as a religious shepherd and guide. He in this manner becomes qualified to benefit them, far beyond what it would be practicable or desirable to do by means of personal familiar intercourse. It is not without reason, that the Apostle gives repeated counsel, that every elder or parochial bishop, should be "the husband of one wife," neither more nor less.

After Mr. Cotton had spent three years in

Boston, his deep and devout studies brought him to a solemn conviction, that there were many antiquated corruptions yet left unreformed in the national Church, with the practice of which he could not comply. From this time, he ceased to conform strictly to the Church of England, though he never voluntarily renounced its communion.

The next chapter will be devoted to an account of the origin and nature of Puritanism, of which John Cotton was a staunch and uncompromising advocate.

CHAPTER III.

Necessity of Controversy. Necessity of Reforming the Church. Romish corruption had taken away Christ's threefold office. Reformation in England restored his prophetical and priestly offices. His kingly office not restored. Relics of Popery retained in the National Church. Puritans demand a complete Reformation. The *principle* involved Nehushtan. How the principles of Congregationalism are reached. Puritans persecuted. Their conduct under persecution. Take refuge in New England. Happy results of their removal. The charge of Schism triumphantly retorted. The Massachusetts settlers no separatists. Laud, the great schismatic. His party were the separatists. Address from the Arbella. The "standing order" in New England no "sect." Puritanism as necessary now as in the days of our fathers. Appeal to the sons of the Pilgrims.

The Puritans lived in an age of controversy. It was one of those periods when the vast sea of human opinions, convulsed under chafing winds and weltering waves, sweeps away many of the ancient landmarks, and often, by their removal, restores to their forgotten prominence such landmarks as are more ancient than they. It was a time when the earthquakes of political and religious agitation disturbed every existing institution; throwing all their foundations out of course, that they might settle down at last upon a basis more firm and square. Novel errors assailed old truths, and new truths grappled with antiquated errors. Perhaps there has never been a waking up of the human mind so general and so intense, as during that prolonged season of every kind of conflict. Such seasons must result in the advancement of truth, the progress of the human mind, and the improvement of the social state. Truth is ultimately, always stronger than her foes. Whatever may be the incidental evils of controversy, they are not so great as the evils it prevents or does away. It is a sharp remedy: but it is less painful than the diseases which it checks or heals. Such keen debate is only to be regretted as altogether injurious, when it arrays the real friends of truth against each other in disputes about matters of inferior moment. In such cases the acrimony is usually in an inverse ratio to the importance of the point discussed. We may then exclaim in the language of the "facetious Fuller," alluding to a passage in the prophet Joel;—"Alas! that men should have less wisdom than locusts, which, when sent on God's errand, *did not thrust one another.*"

The necessity of reform in the church arose from its corruption. The leaven of this corruption had begun to work even before the decease of the apostles.* And from that time, the spreading fermentation, diffusing itself through a long course of ages, at last leavened nearly the whole mass with the sour crudities of popery. No doubt, the church as yet unreformed was the true church, just as a tree decayed and maimed is still a true tree. But there was need that the dead limbs should be lopped down, and the rotten wood cut out, and the eating funguses removed, and the encroaching mosses and other hurtful parasites scraped off, and the heterogeneous grafts pruned away. In short, there was much that wanted to be done, to restore the aged tree to a natural and vigorous growth, without amputating any part that retained its health and soundness. It was not the design of the reformers to institute a new church : but to restore the integrity and purity of the old. And so far as it experienced such reformation, it is primitive, apostolical and catholic.

Antichrist had so far prevailed, as greatly to interfere with the sole Headship of Christ in and over his church. His threefold office of chief Prophet, high Priest, and only King, had been dangerously and ruinously invaded. The light of the gospel, obscured by foggy ignorance

* 2 Thess. 2: 7.

and fuming errors, had left the world in darkness.

> "O blindness of our earth-incrusted minds!
> In what a midnight shade, what sombrous clouds
> Of error, are our souls immersed, when Thou,
> O Sun supreme, no longer deign'st to shine!"

Welcome, thunder:—and welcome, hurricane;—if those gloomy, fatal clouds are thereby swept away. Luther, wake the storm, that the heavens may be cleared; and the Sun of Righteousness shine forth in his strength!

Christ's *prophetical* office, as the authoritative teacher of his Church, had been infringed by substituting the teachings and traditions of men in the place of his instructions. The pure doctrines of his Word were no longer taught or understood. Dogmas wholly subversive of them were received instead. The grace which redeems and renews the sinner, and which it is the main design of the Bible to inculcate, was lost sight of. Nothing was regarded but such matters as the efficacy of penance and indulgences, the nature of purgatory and transubstantiation, and other things as contrary to the lessons of the Bible as Belial is to the Christ of God.

The *priestly* office of Jesus, who is the only atoning sacrifice and the one Mediator between God and men, was no less invaded. The doctrine that human merit can avail to purchase salvation displaced that most fundamental article of Christianity, that remission of sins and the gift of eternal life is through faith alone. It was held, that the sacraments of themselves had power to sanctify the recipients; although the gospel denies all efficacy to forms and ceremonies, aside from the special influence of the Holy Spirit. Other mediators with God were set up by the side of Jesus, and even above him, in the affection and confidence of the worshipers. Full faith was given to all manner of absurd miracles, alledged to be wrought by hermits, and departed saints, and other celestial beings.

"Such tales monastic fablers taught,
Their kindred strain the minstrels caught;
A web of finer texture they
Wrought from the rich romantic lay."

The virgin mother; with a host of martyrs of all sorts, real and fabulous; with numberless saints, many of them of uncertain existence, and others of very dubious sanctity; with good spirits and legendary angels: all these were relied upon in vows and prayers, to the injury of the Redeemer's exclusive right to stand and intercede between the sinner and his God.

These infractions of his claims were attended by the usurpation of Christ's *kingly* office. In despite of his just prerogative to be supreme Head and Lawgiver in his own kingdom, men, assuming to act by his authority, dared to set aside his laws, and supplant them by ordinances of their own invention. The Son of God had prescribed the terms of membership and communion in the church which he had purchased with his own blood, and the mode of dealing with offenders: he had deposited with the church the sacred "power of the keys" wherewith to bind and loose: he had indicated the character of the officers under his government, and defined the nature of their authority and their duties: and he had stamped upon his worship and ordinances a simplicity becoming to their spiritual character. But a usurping hierarchy, engrossing a power belonging to none but Christ, had overturned all his enactments; and instituted ceremonies and modes of worship utterly foreign to his will; and imposed terms of communion and office in the church, totally repugnant to the divinely appointed order and discipline of the house of God.

Such were the gross abuses and corruptions which had long prevailed, before the Protestant Reformation,—that moral equator of the world's history. It had become necessary to "prove all things;" and rejecting the evil, to hold fast to that which is good. One of the old divines has correctly said:—"The reformers disclaimed only the ulcers and sores, not what was sound in the existing church."

Now in England, during the reigns of the eighth Henry and some of his next successors, the needful reformation had advanced so far as to terminate the open infractions of Christ's prophetical and priestly offices. The doctrines he taught were openly professed once more: and free salvation by his atonement and intercession was now preached again.

But here the work came to a stand. The invasions of the royal and legislative office of the Saviour were not redressed. The only alteration was a change of usurpers. The pope and his myrmidons were cast out only to make room for another set who claimed to be heads and lawmakers to that city of God, which owed allegiance and obedience in these matters to the Lord alone.

The Anglican Church had never been thoroughly purged from the remnants of popery. They, who first took the work in hand, were not able, in consequence of the premature death of the sixth Edward, to carry it on so far as they intended. And such as came after them strove rather, so far as they could, to retrace their steps toward the recently forsaken Babylon. It was not without reason that one of the divines of the Church of England exclaimed :—" What need hath reformation itself to be frequently reformed, seeing corruptions will so quickly creep thereinto." That Church retained so much of the essence of popery, that Rome, to this day, has never given up the hope that her vagrant daughter will yet return to her embraces. Says Edward Weston, a Jesuit in the time of Henry VIII ;—" The English drove the pope out of the kingdom so hastily, that they forced him to leave his garments behind him : and now they put them on, and, like so many players acting their parts, they dance in them in a way of triumph." And the bloody Bonner, then Bishop of London, playfully remarked, in allusion to the superstitions which were retained ;—" If they sup of our broth, they will soon eat of our beef !" The archbishop of Spalato, who came to England in 1616, declares in a letter to bishop Hall, that he saw nothing reformed there but the bare doctrine of the church. It is not strange, therefore, that a strong tendency toward Rome has been ever betraying itself in that quarter. Bishop Taylor considered his church to be separated from that of Rome merely by " a paper wall." And though some excellent men have affirmed that the said paper wall was "just the thickness of the Bible," other men have found no difficulty in surmounting it, and getting back into the Italian fold. The church theory of the Anglicans is the same as that of the Romanists. Both communions are based upon the same pretensions: they rest alike on that ecclesiastical figment, which is miscalled "apostolical succession." If this be a good reason for being a prelatist, it is a far stronger reason for being a papist. The pope urges the same arguments against the prelatists, that these latter use against us: and the same reasons justify us for disowning the supremacy of the prelates, which justify them for disowning the supremacy of the pope. It is natural that the high churchmen of England and elsewhere should sigh for such a reconciliation as might procure an endorsement of their claims by the pretended successors to St. Peter's chair. It is easy to understand the zeal of the Oxford divines, whose labors threaten to give occasion for renewing the complaint of archbishop Laud, "a man whom it is an act of self-denial to name without some epithet of reproach." In his dying speech, he said;—"The Church of England is become like an oak, cleft to shivers with wedges made out of its own body."

John Cotton, and other Puritans, regarded the

Church of England as wofully dissenting from the true Church of Christ, by her making the monarch of the realm her head and ruler. The king of Britain, say they, is a "protestant in taking, not in giving." Honest Fuller says;—"The pope being dead in England, the king was found his heir at common law, as to most of the power and profit the other had usurped." This impious intrusion of an earthly prince, who might oftentimes be a monster of profligacy, or perhaps a mere child, a girl, into the throne of Zion's King, was more than the Puritans, ever jealous for the rights and honors of their Lord, could brook. They felt that "the church by law established" had dissented from the true basis of the church of God, because her articles of faith and frame of government rested on acts of parliament, which has power to new model her at will: whereas she should have stood upon the simple foundation of the Word of God. Osborne observes, in his Memoirs of Queen Elizabeth;—"The doctrine professed most generally in England, bore in foreign nations the name of parliament faith."* This phrase often occurs in the letters of Erasmus.

Now the Puritans demanded, in the name of

* Parliamentaria fides.

the Lord, that his royal power and privilege should be restored to him. New England had her "judicious Hooker," him of Hartford, the fellow-voyager with John Cotton to these shores. This good man thus explains the object sought by himself and his brethren;—"As the *prophetical* and *priestly* office of Christ, was completely vindicated in the first times of reformation, so now the great cause and work of God's reforming people is, to clear the rights of Christ's *kingly* office, and in their practice to set up his kingdom."* They received the name of *Puritans* from their resolute attempt to restore to their primitive *purity* the Christian faith and institutions, according to the principles laid down by the adorable Founder of Christianity. Their sentiments are thus expressed by the celebrated Dr. John Owen:—"They who hold communion with the Lord Jesus Christ, will admit nothing, practice nothing, in the worship of God, but what they have his warrant for. Unless coming in his name, they will not hear an angel from heaven. They know the apostles themselves were to teach the saints only what he commanded them. And you know how many in this very nation, in the days not long since

* Preface to Survey of Church Discipline.

passed, yea, how many thousands left their native soil, and went into a vast and howling wilderness, in the uttermost parts of the world, to keep their souls undefiled and chaste unto their dear Lord Jesus, as to this matter of his worship and institutions."*

It is necessary that we should understand the *principle* involved in this great controversy. The Puritans did not contend for the abolishing of a few harmless or insignificant ceremonies more or less. They were willing, in the main, that such as chose to practice them voluntarily should do so. But they resisted the arbitrary imposition of those ceremonies upon those who conscientiously disliked them. And they resisted the imposition of such things as conditions of membership and ministry in the church, chiefly because they abrogated the only conditions which Christ had seen fit to establish, and presumed to bring in others by the force of human enactments. They held, that the attempt to annul the terms of citizenship and office which Christ had decreed in his spiritual kingdom, and to substitute and enforce others of human devising, was an act of usurpation, and essentially treasonable and rebellious against the King of Zion.

* Communion with God.

To comprehend the merits of this controversy, we are not to look at the importance of the points objected to in the forms of the national church, considered in themselves. In itself, it may be of very little consequence, whether, or not, ordination shall be exclusively performed by diocesans,—or whether or not the sign of the cross shall be used in baptism,—or whether the externals of public worship shall be performed in one way or another way,—or whether the Lord's Supper shall be received in this posture or in that. These, it may be, are small questions to divide the church about. And yet it argues much more of smallness of soul to insist that they shall always be answered in one particular way, as did the prelatical party, than to insist that every one should enjoy his own preference in such matters, according to the free spirit of Christianity, as did the Puritans. They cared the less whether these things were essential or not. But it became a question of awful magnitude, when they began to ask, By what right do men, setting aside the regulations of Christ, assume to say;—"Conform to our canons and decrees, albeit your Lord has never enjoined them: else you shall have no place in the house of God!" In this imperious demand, the Puritans saw not only an act of grievous tyranny over the consciences of the disciples, the free-born children of the house; but they beheld an appalling invasion of the exclusive rights and dignities of the Lord and Master of the household. It was not merely against the unrighteous exclusion of faithful men from the communion of the church and its covenanted mercies, against which our fathers protested; but it was much more against proceedings so derogatory to the glory of the Mediator's throne. Even such trivial affairs as crucifixes and surplices acquire a magnitude not properly belonging to them, when they trench upon our allegiance to the Prince of life. Let it cost what it will, the supreme and undivided sovereignty and headship of Christ over all things pertaining to the church must be preserved inviolate and entire.

Our later fathers, in the revolutionary times, acted like sound political puritans. Those staunch *Boston boys* did not make one great teapot of our harbor, and tinge its waters, as we say, with that greenish cerulean hue which it has never lost:—they did not thus hasten the glorious independence of these colonies, because they were too penurious to pay for the Chinese leaf three pence in the pound more than was proper. Oh no:—it was because they withstood the odious and tyrannical principle of taxation without representation. They stood for the right which, Burke says, "the Anglo-Saxon race have claimed in all ages, of being taxed only with their own consent." They were readier to die than to submit to this paltry import duty: for they saw that it was designed to sanction a practice which must wrest from them the most cherished of their British liberties, and bring in a thousand forms of oppression upon them and their posterity.

Possibly, some of the ceremonies of the church may have been once innocent, and even useful, like the venerable sign of the cross. But when, by long abuse, they had come to be inseparably coupled with superstition, there was good cause why the observance of them, at least the *compulsory* observance, should cease. Among the commendable actions of the pious Hezekiah, we read that he "brake in pieces the brazen serpent that Moses had made; for unto those days, the children of Israel did burn incense to it; and he called it, Nehushtan;"—that is, a mere piece of brass. Now this was a most precious relic of antiquity. By means of it, God had wrought a most wonderful deliverance for his people. It was even a type of the Messiah himself, who should yet be uplifted by the gospel, even "as Moses lifted up that serpent in the wilderness," so that perishing souls might look to him and live. And yet the Jewish king, like a godly and zealous Puritan, as in his time he was, dashed it to fragments, that it should no more be perverted to idolatrous purposes. They who approve this deed, which God himself approved, cannot but justify the image-breaking of our fathers.

The church had become encrusted with many successive *layers of corrupt innovation.* For ages, these accretions had been forming one upon another. The wish of the Puritans was, to peel off these lamina ; and to remove them all, till they should come down to the original proper substance of the Church. They were for unwinding the interminable mummy-cloths, by which the Church had been nearly bandaged into a corpse ; and so restoring her to life and enjoyment, to beauty and action. They followed the plan of stripping off all those usages which could not plead the recorded inspiration of the Bible in their favor. They rejected every canon and custom, of whose origin they could tell the date, and of whose originators they could give the names. And when all these foreign, uncongenial and injurious inventions, which had been superimposed upon the primitive discipline, had been removed, they found as the result, our noble Congregational Church Polity. Take any existing Church, and deprive it of all the peculiarities for which it is indebted to man, until nothing is left but what is of divine institution, and the pure Scriptural residuum, thus purged of human adulterations, will be simple Congregationalism. This system of Church polity, perfectly accords with the genius of Christianity, and is instinct with the free spirit of our religion.

For reducing their views on the subject of Church government to practice, and for acting in accordance with their convictions, it is well known that our fathers were very roughly handled by those who claimed to be their ecclesiastical superiors. The persecuted men submitted to their sufferings for the Lord's sake. It was no part of their policy, to conduct themselves so outrageously, as, in a manner, to compel magistrates to restrain, or mobs to assail them. They did not first by their misbehavior, necessitate a tumultuous opposition; and then raise a piteous cry of "Persecution! persecution!" The plan of trading in this sort of capital, and making their gains out of the sympathy of a silly multitude led away by such tricks of "moral reform," was an invention of after times. When it could be avoided, our fathers shunned the stroke of oppression, and shielded themselves in every justifiable way. But when it was inevitable, they met it calmly and courageously, they bore it meekly and piously, as the chastening of the Lord. In Luther's "Table Discourses," we find that bold reformer saying;—"When governors and rulers are enemies to God's word, then our duty is to depart, to sell or forsake all we have, to fly from one place to another, as Christ commandeth. We must make and prepare no uproars and tumults, by reason of the gospel; but we must suffer all things."

Thus did the Puritans. When a parish minister in England, found any of the practices of the National Church to be contrary to the simplicity and obedience of Christ, he discontinued the use of them. He abandoned one such point after another, as fast as his conscience was enlightened in respect to them. Meanwhile, he kept quietly along in the discharge of all his ministerial functions. If the ecclesiastical powers took no notice of his non-conformity as to their unrighteous regulations, as was often the case for considerable periods together, the man of God labored peacefully and zealously for the salvation of the flock committed to his care, by the providence of the great Head of the Church. When at last the vigilant eye of official despotism, took notice of his Puritanism, he sought to screen himself from the coming storm, by calling to his aid such protectors as he could find. When such means failed, and warrants were issued for his arrest and imprisonment, he then "fled from one city to another;" he either concealed himself among friends, till the tempest should blow over, or strove to escape through ports strictly guarded to prevent his departure, and live as an exile in some foreign land. But if he fell into the hands of those who would lord it over a conscience which refused obedience in spiritual matters to any but Christ, he then submitted with dignified resignation, to the pains and penalties of the law. He refused to renounce his Master; but he refused not to suffer for him. Of such, some, subjected to fines and confiscations, "took joyfully the spoiling of their goods;" "and others had trial of cruel mockings and scourgings, yea, moreover of bonds and imprisonment;" and others still "refused not to die, for the name of the Lord Jesus."

When extruded from their parish churches, they met, in retired places, such part of their flocks as sought their instructions, with a love for the truth which surmounted the sense of peril; for the arm of power sought to suppress these "conventicles," as they were opprobriously termed. And yet, originally, this was a most honorary name; for the primitive churches were called "conventicles," by the pagan emperors, in those days when the Roman sword dripped with an unceasing stream of martyr's blood.*

When driven forth as banished men, our fathers did not feel that they were forsaking the sacred cause of the gospel. Their exile to these western shores was a confession that the faith was dearer to them, than all the cherished objects of attachment they left behind. They thus evinced how much they "preferred Jerusalem above their chief joy." They regarded their exodus from the land of bondage, as "not a flight *from* duty, but *unto* duty." Here they were enabled to bear a more decided testimony against the intermixture of human inventions, with divine ordinances, than they could have done elsewhere. Here only, could they maintain in their purity, the worship and polity of the gospel. We see the wisdom of God in transplanting them to these vacant deserts, whose remoteness made them more fit for free and untrammeled inquiry for the ordinances of the Bible. Here no antiquated prejudices rudely thwarted the investigating mind. No frowning cathedral, with gloomy pomp, predisposed the mind of the worshiper to accord with usages,

* Arnobius, Lib. 4. Ed. Lugd., p. 152. Lactantius, Inst. Lib. 5. c. 11. De Morte Persec. cc. 15, 34, 36, 48.

which, for centuries, had obscured the evangelical sincerity. Amid the aisles of the forest, and beneath the dome of heaven, surrounded by nature in its pristine state, as yet, untouched by art; environed by the works of the Creator, which the hands of man had not assayed to remodel, our fathers reverently hearkened to the oracles of God. In this temple not made with hands, they first celebrated that worship, which is not of mere human appointment. It was thus, in the wilderness, that God gave to Moses the pattern of the tabernacle. It was while he was an exile in an uncultured part of Chaldea, that Ezekiel saw the plan of the temple. It was during his banishment to the desert isle of Patmos, that the Apostle beheld that glorious vision of the city of God. And it was amid these primeval solitudes, that God more distinctly manifested to our pilgrim sires, the true frame and model of the primitive Church. Here they afforded a specimen of the new heavens and the new earth, "which, according to his promise, we look for."

For having obeyed their consciences, which bid them obey the Bible,—for having followed the leading of the Scripture, which is at once the two-edged sword and royal sceptre of the Son of God in his spiritual kingdom,—for refusing to keep the commandments and traditions of men,—the Puritans have been covered with reproaches. Especially have they been charged with the odious accusation of separation from the true Church of God; breaking out of her enclosure, and casting themselves, in all the presumption of unbelief, on the uncovenanted mercies of God. No pains have been spared to heap scorn upon their name, and to brand them with the odious crime of *schism.*

But this charge of schism they hurled back, like Abdiel replying to the prince of darkness, "with retorted scorn." One of them, speaking of the Laudians, and their triple plot of Arminianism, Romanism, and civil Despotism, for the promotion of all which they so furiously urged conformity, makes the following strong remarks: "We dare not be guilty of the schism which we charge upon that party in the Church of England; and if any faction of men will require the assent and consent of other men to a vast number of disputable and uninstituted things, and utterly renounce all christian communion with all that shall not give that assent and consent, we look upon *those* to be separatists."

The Puritans did not consider themselves as excluded from communion by the Church of England, but by a schismatical faction which had gotten the upper hand in that communion. They ever insisted that they were true and faithful sons of that ancient Church: "nor did they think it was their *mother* who turned them out of doors," but some of their mother's *children* who were angry with them, and who, abusing the name of their mother, so harshly treated them. They held, that the true Protestant Reforming Church of England, comprehended all faithful, baptized Christians, however variant, as to modes of belief and practice in lesser points of religion, and wherever dispersed, throughout the then British dominions. This holy and catholic fellowship they steadfastly maintained.

They felt that it was unjust and libelous, that they should be stigmatized as Schismatics, merely because they were determined, as Christians ought to be, to allow of no unauthorized intrusion upon the kingly office of their Lord. They were sensible, that they were grossly wronged in being treated as heretics, only for conforming to the will of Christ, instead of the will of man; and for seeking to restore the sacred streams of ecclesiastical usage to the primitive channels, from whence they had been drawn aside into so many branching canals by the innovators of a dozen centuries. The Puritans agreed with Bishop Stillingfleet in the preface to his Irenicum, that Christ, "who came to take away the insupportable yoke of the Jewish ceremonies, certainly did never intend to gall the necks of disciples with another, instead of it; and it would be strange, if the church would require more than Christ himself did; and make more terms of communion, than our Saviour did of discipleship." "The grand commission the apostles were sent out with, was only to teach *what Christ had commanded them;* not the least intimation of any power given them to impose or require any thing, beyond what he himself had spoken to them, or they were directed to by the immediate guidance of the Spirit of God." To the statutes of Christ, promulgated by the inspired Apostles, the Puritans ever gladly submitted. Though they refused to subscribe to parliament canons, they were always ready to subscribe to the New Testament. When Archbishop Laud undertook to cut off such members from the Church, our fathers regarded him as a man who should bestride one bough of a tree, and fall to sawing it off between himself and the main-trunk, under pretence of lopping off the whole tree! They looked upon Laud as the grand Schismatic, who was destined to catch a severe fall as the result of his sectarizing operations. The last stroke of his axe, he felt in his own person, at what time the oppressed rose up in desperation, "and wronged the wronger till he rendered right."

There are many good reasons which will justify a man for transferring his covenant relation from one true church, to another such. No exception can be taken at the opinion of Dr. Ames;—"If any, wronged with unjust vexation, or providing for his own edification, or in testimony against sin, depart from a church where some evils are tolerated, and join himself to another more pure, yet without condemning the church he leaveth, he is not therefore to be held as a schismatic, or as guilty of any other sin."* To leave even a pure church, for one comparatively more pure, provided it be done with due love and respect toward the body which is left, is no rupture of spiritual unity, or breach of Zion's peace. "Unity in diversity, and diversity in unity,—is a law of nature, and also of the Church." Though every tent-pin which really belongs to the tabernacle, is hallowed and precious, we should not break the cords, or rend the curtains to pieces, for the sake of driving every pin with the utmost exactness.

The guilt of schism, where it is actually in-

* Book of Conscience, Book iv: ch. xiv. no 16.

curred, is terrible indeed. It is hateful in the sight of the Lord. More rude than the soldiers at the cross, it rends asunder his seamless vesture. Nay in its wilder and more savage excesses, it would fix its demon clutches on his sacred and mystical body, to rend it, if that were possible, limb from limb.

Now if there were any schism involved in the wide division of sentiments between the Puritans, and the domineering heads who were then lording it over God's heritage, we contend that the fault lay wholly with the latter. They refused to part with the popish relics which still hung thick about the "Church by law established," and which the first reformers had only left for a season, till the state of public opinion among the body of the people should be sufficiently enlightened to permit the entire abolition of them. Though the time had come when these vestiges of popery might have been peacefully thrown off, the Laudians not only clung tenaciously to them, but used every exertion to restore as much as possible of the accursed Babylonish vesture which had been cast aside. The Puritans, who "hated even the *garments spotted* by the flesh" of the idolatrous Church of Rome, contracted no schismatic taint by their endeavors to escape all contact with so much as one polluted shred worn by that *ancient harlot* who had reveled so long on the spoils of Christ's kingdom, and made herself drunk with the blood of her saints. Well were they vindicated in a speech of the eloquent Chatham, in the house of Lords, in 1773. Dr. Drummond, archbishop of York, had taxed the non-conforming clergy as men of "close ambition." "They are so, my lords," retorted the noble earl, "and their ambition is to keep close to the college of fishermen, not of cardinals; and to the doctrine of inspired apostles, not to the decrees of interested and aspiring bishops. They contend for a spiritual creed and a spiritual worship; we have a Calvinistic creed, a popish liturgy, and an Arminian clergy." Sure it was no sin for the Puritans to do their best to bring the church out of such an unnatural and unreasonable predicament, even if it could only be effected by a remedy adequate to the disease,—another Protestant reformation.

But we take stronger ground than this, in vindicating our conscientious fathers from the sin of schism. They did not willfully and willingly withdraw from the communion of the parish churches of England. As Chillingworth says, they were "*non fugitivi, sed fugati;*" they were not voluntary fugitives, but were driven to compulsory flight. They were not spontaneous seceders; they were expelled by force and power. They would have remained in the folds wherein they were born, had they been suffered to do so, except on the impossible condition of defiling their consciences and violating the Word of God. They may have trembled somewhat at the menaces of the great; but they trembled much more at the Word of the Lord. They were willing that others should conform, who could do it without hurting their own consciences. Even Luther could say;—"I could be well content to hold the pope in befitting respect and honor, yet so far that he permitted me to have my conscience at liberty, and forced me not to offend my God, and to act any thing against him."

But the non-conformists of England were not allowed to abide in the national church, nor even in the realm, except on the hard alternative of conforming to what they felt to be sin, or else inhabiting the prisons. They went not forth of their own accord; they were thrust out at the sword's point. It was thus that they became "strangers unto their brethren, and aliens unto their mother's children." Who, then, were the schismatics?—the men, who, willing to tolerate others, refused to sin against the sole supremacy of Christ in his Church?—or they who imposed unscriptural terms of communion, and exacted strict conformity as the price of toleration? Says Hales of Eaton;—"Where cause of schism is necessary, there, not he that separates, but he that occasions the separation, is schismatic."* We cannot but think that the sin of schism, if any there be, cleaves to the tyrannous and imperious exactors of things which Christ has never commanded; and not to the pious recusants. To these last may well be applied the parting benediction of Moses;—"Let the blessing come upon the head of Joseph, and upon the top of the head of him that was separated from his brethren."

The year 1662 is forever memorable in the annals of the suffering non-conformists. Then was passed and enforced the infamous act of uniformity, which deserves to be classed with the rescripts which caused the Bartholomew massacres, and with the revocation of the edict of Nantes. That act of uniformity was the dividing stroke of separation, and it was not dealt by the hands of the Puritans, but by those of their relentless oppressors. Jonathan Mitchell was then pastor of Cambridge in New England: a man of whom Baxter said;—"If there could be convened an œcumenical council of the whole

* Tract concerning schism, in Sparks' Collection, v. 25.

Christian world, that man would be worthy to be the moderator of it.* On the last day of that eventful year, the matchless Mitchell, as his friends loved to call him, wrote as follows;— "Our cause is not separation from any thing good in other churches, whether truth of church-state, or any doctrine rightly professed, or ordinance rightly administered in them. But it is reformation only of what is amiss or defective in the churches we came from.† This defines the true position of our fathers: a position which none will assail, but those who fancy that "healing the sores must maim the body."

When Moses, descending from the mount, found the catholic congregation of Israel turned to idolatry, he "took the tabernacle, and pitched it without the camp, afar off from the camp, and called it the Tabernacle of the Congregation." In this, be sure, he was not guilty of schism; and much less were our fathers, when going forth on compulsion, unwilling exiles, they took the tabernacle, made in all things according to the pattern showed them in the mount, and set it up, far from the camp of idolatry, in this western wilderness. As the followers of Jesus, who,

* Remarkables of Dr. I. Mather.

† Elijah's Mantle, p. 2.

"that he might sanctify the people with his own blood, suffered without the gate," their language was;—"Let us go forth unto him without the camp, bearing his reproach; for here have we no continuing city, but we seek one to come." Jesus was in his time a great reformer and Puritan, coming with his winnowing fan in his hand, that he might thoroughly purge his floor: and such schismatics as he and his apostles were when cast out of the synagogues of Judea, even such were our fathers when forcibly extruded from the parish churches of England.

That they suffered this extrusion solely against their will, and therefore were not accountable for it, as being a misery they could not avoid, is manifest from many proofs. It appears in that celebrated and pathetic address sent by the first Massachusetts emigrants while yet on board the Arbella, "to the rest of their brethren in and of the Church of England." "We are not of those," say that noble band, "who dream of perfection in this world; yet we desire that you would be pleased to take notice of the principals and body of our company, as those who esteem it our honor to call the Church of England, from whence we rise, our dear mother, and cannot part from our native country where she specially resideth, without much sadness of heart, and many tears in our eyes; ever acknowledging that such hope and part as we have obtained in the common salvation, we have received in her bosom, and sucked it from her breasts. We leave it not, therefore, as loathing that milk wherewith we were nourished there; but blessing God for the parentage and education, as members of the same body, shall always rejoice in her good, and unfeignedly grieve for any sorrow that shall ever betide her; and while we have breath, sincerely desire and endeavor the continuance and abundance of her welfare, with the enlargement of her bounds in the kingdom of Christ Jesus; wishing our heads and hearts were fountains of tears for your everlasting welfare, when we shall be in our poor cottages in the wilderness, overshadowed with the spirit of supplication."* So too, the year before, the pious Higginson, the faithful pastor of Salem, in taking his last look of his native land from the stern of his ship, exclaimed;—" We will not say as the Separatists were wont to say at their leaving of England, Farewell, Babylon! Farewell, Rome! But we will say, Farewell, dear England! Farewell, the Church of God in England, and all the Christian friends there! We

* Hubbard, Chapter XXIII.

do not go to New England as separatists from the Church of England; though we cannot but separate from the corruptions in it: but we go to practice the positive part of church reformation, and propagate the gospel in America."*

Jonathan Mitchell, at whose untimely death it was said, that "all New England shook when that pillar fell to the ground," thus expressed the matter in his sermon, called "Nehemiah upon the Wall." Speaking against "separation, anabaptism and anarchial confusion," he says;—"If any would secretly twist in, and espouse such things as those, and make them part of our *interest*, we must needs renounce it as none of *our cause*, no part of the end and design of the Lord's faithful servants, when they followed him "into this land that was not sown." Separation and anabaptism, are wonted intruders, and seeming friends, but secret fatal enemies, to reformation. Do not, on pretence of avoiding corruption, run into sinful separation from any true churches of God, and what is *good* therein. And yet it is our errand into the wilderness to study and practice true Scripture reformation; and it will be our crown in the sight of God and man, if we find it and hold it, without adulterating deviations."

* Magnalia, Book III., ch. I., Sec. 12.

Additional testimonies of the same character will be given in another place. Such language must fully exculpate such as used it from the charge of making schismatical divisions, if it be admitted that they uttered these expressions with sincerity. We are too well aware, that some mean and malignant writers, who were unable to conceive it possible that men could entertain such magnanimous sentiments as these, have questioned the sincerity of our fathers. The character of our fathers, so bold to avow the truth, and so resolute to suffer in its behalf, sufficiently refutes the calumny. The most decided Congregationalists among their descendants, whose sincerity has never been questioned, read the above cited declarations of Winthrop and his associates with high approbation, and heartily accord with the sentiments therein expressed. The New England churches consider themselves to be purified branches of that original church-stock which flourished in England, before Romish art and violence had twisted it out of its proper shape and form.

Surely it is the extremity of injustice to accuse the Puritans as being of a schismatical temper. They felt themselves, as we, their descendants, and inheritors of their principles, now feel ourselves to be, in full fellowship with all that is good and all that is true in the communion of the Church of England and in every other Christian denomination. They and we are inseparably joined to the whole church catholic of faithful men, "endeavoring to keep the unity of the Spirit in the bond of peace."

The multiplicity of sects is much deplored. A *sect*, according to the derivation of the word, is something which is "cut off." But in New England, the "standing order," is no sect, no cut-off. We are not dissected from others, even though they be severed from us. We be the main-stock, which remains rooted and grounded, even when parted branches are torn away. We are the mother-church, and so no flying off of her children, can make us as any one of them. Whatever other respected denominations and beloved sister-churches may be, we are here, no sect,—no cut-off; but the original vine of God's planting in this land. We grow upon the ancient trunk, "partaking of its root and fatness." We be no innovators, no revolutionists, no disorganizers. Our church polity, and scheme of doctrine, is in rightful possession of all the ground it holds.

Thus, if we insist upon the use of the Bible in our common Schools, we set up no novel claim. This country was settled by Bible

Christians, who spent life and treasure for the purpose of making the Bible the basis of our system of education, as well as of all the rest of our social institutions. We are only on defensive and conservative ground, and are only moving on in the straightforward track of duty.

We have showed the necessity of Puritanism in the days of our fathers,—the need of thorough ecclesiastical reform in regard to the infringements and usurpal encroachments upon Christ's kingly office in the government of the Church he had purchased with his own blood. In this point of view, they were the light of the world, and shone serene, far above the troubled clouds, which by snatches obscured their brightness from the sight of men.

Yes: the Puritan piety was needed in that day. And no less is it needed now. The words of one of those good men are as seasonable as ever;—"Babylon paints her face anew at this day; antichrist hath varnished his interest, so that there are many who are allured and taken with the beauty of that harlot." We have also seen the truth of his further remark, that "a loose protestant is fit to become a strict papist."* Human corruption is seeking as

* W. Stoughton, Election Sermon, 1668. p. 27.

busily as ever, to obscure the beaming simplicity of the gospel; spoiling its divine beauty "through philosophy and vain deceit, after the tradition of men, after the rudiments of the world, and not after Christ." Alas for our Zion, once "the perfection of beauty, the joy of the whole earth," alas for her, if that race of noble spirits shall become extinct in such a day of rebuke and blasphemy as this. "The fathers,—where are they?"

> "O, they are fled the light! Those mighty spirits
> Lie raked up with their ashes in their urns;
> And not a spark of their eternal fire,
> Glows in a present bosom."

But no;—the sacred flame is not quenched in this land, which the prayers of our pilgrim sires have hallowed, and made it holy ground.

> "E'en in their ashes, live their wonted fires."

The latent heat pervades the soil, breathes genially in the air, and diffuses the life-warmth through all our social state.

Our thoughts revert to those days of sorest trial, when our fathers and mothers literally "left all," to follow Christ into "a land not sown." "Weep not for the dead, neither bemoan him; but weep sore for him that goeth away; for he shall return no more, nor see his native country." What a scene the embarkation of those sorrowing companies of pilgrims must have been. There were godly and reverend ministers, disguised in shipman's garb, apprehensively watching, lest the pursuivant should come to arrest their flight; dreading to go, but dreading more to be hindered from going. There were men with anxious countenances, hurrying the preparations for their tedious voyage;—women, with care-worn features, and looks of resignation, waiting the last signal in silent agony:—children, poor things, who must be borne far away, not knowing whither or why. There were friends to be left behind, under the sad presentiment of meeting no more on earth. The tenderest ties were sundering, even such as had never been severed before. Were there ever sorrows or tears like those? What impassioned repetitions of terms of endearment, such as excited affection loves to utter, were mutually breathed, till the voice became choked with emotion, and they wept upon each other's necks till they recovered speech again. Then comes the breaking away from fond embraces, whose tender pressure shall never again be felt;—the brief farewells, the ejaculated blessings, the affectionate charges, and messages of love to absent friends. And now the last fast is cast off. The vessel moves upon her billowy course. The forms so tearfully watched, recede into fainter view. But waving signals tell of the "longing, lingering glances," which cannot bear the deep desponding anguish of the last—last look.

O love of Jesus! how does it triumph in such an hour of bitterest woe! O the power of religion, which can constrain to a living martyrdom, keen as the pangs of death, and torturing as the cross! Aye, how does it cheer the soul, not by stupifying its sensibilities, but by lifting them all torn and bleeding, to the view of a pitying Saviour, and elevated in sublime devotion, receiving from his compassion, a rush of sympathy, an overflowing consolation, a joy so full of heaven, that earth and all its sorrows are sweetly forgotten. Blessed wounds which bring such healing! Happy griefs which teach such comfort! These scars of the heart are the love-tokens of Christ, and the treasured pledges of a home whose friendships are eternal, and where parting is unknown.

Let us rally around the banner of our sires. What recreant and caitive heart, what degenerate spirit would desert it now? The pilgrims bore it, like valiant standard-bearers, in the front of the Lord's battle. There it has ever been wont to fly, where the conflict raged strongest against the powers of darkness. And still untorn and untarnished, it has often waved over the field of its glorious triumphs. Though the flag, in these stiller times, may hang drooping from the lofty staff, yet, when iniquity cometh in like a flood, the Spirit of the Lord, as a rushing, mighty wind, shall lift up the ancient standard. Then, in sure token of victory, it will spread out its ample folds, with the broad blazon of the bannered cross.

CHAPTER IV.

Mr. Cotton countenanced by the people in his non-conformity. Suspension from ministry. Suspension unexpectedly taken off. Successful labors. Theological instructions. Indefatigable preaching. Correspondence. Wonderful and general reformation. Archbishop Williams. Earls of Dorchester and Lyndsay. Disabled by ague. Second marriage. Cited to High Commission Court. Fate of the informer. Earl of Dorset intercedes for Mr. Cotton in vain. Concealment. Letter to Mrs. Cotton. Sets out to go to Holland. Diverted to London. Interesting conference with Mr. Davenport and others. Resolves to go to New England. Embarks with difficulty in the Griffin.

When Mr. Cotton ceased from his conformity with the exceptionable features in the national worship, so great was his popularity with his people, that, far from opposing him on that account, the greatest part of them sustained him in his course. Thomas Leverett, however, one of his parishioners, with some others, prosecuted complaints against their minister in the Episcopal courts; till, after some time, he was silenced by order of the bishop.

During his suspension, Mr. Cotton gave constant attendance to the public preaching of his substitute; but never to the reading of the Book of Common Prayer. He was now subjected to severe temptations to swerve from the path of duty. He was not only promised, that he should be restored to the freedom of his ministry, but promoted to very great preferment in the church, on condition of conformity to the scrupled rites, only in a single instance. But he kept the integrity of his conscience undefiled, "unawed by influence, and unbribed by gain." Meanwhile a portentous cloud of troubles was gathering over his head; but was strangely dispersed again. Mr. Leverett himself, the author of these difficulties, became deeply penitent for his agency in causing them. He went to one of the proctors of the archi-episcopal court, to whom he presented a pair of gloves, and then made his appeal from the court below. Mr. Leverett made oath before this officer, who favored him in the terms of the deposition, that "Mr. Cotton was a man conformable *to the mind of the Lord.*" On the strength of this very ambiguous deposition, the silenced minister, he scarce knew how, found himself healed of his ecclesiastical bronchitis, and restored to the use of his voice in the pulpit. The same Mr. Leverett ever after was his steadfast friend; and following his fortunes to this side of the Atlantic, was for many years a useful elder in the first church in Boston, Mass. By the same means, Mr. Bennet, another of his parishioners, occasionally screened his minister from harassing prosecutions.

After this affair, Mr. Cotton went on with his sacred duties, uninterrupted for many years. Making no efforts to build up a party or to gain adherents, he laboriously devoted himself to teaching the people the Christian religion. During the twenty years that he retained his charge, he thrice went over the whole body of systematic divinity, with especial pains to indoctrinate the younger part of his flock. In his preaching he largely expounded several of the books of Scripture, in which gift he greatly excelled.

As one instance of his power to awaken the conscience, it is said that he once handled the sixth commandment with such effect, that a woman who had been married sixteen years to her second husband, openly confessed to the crime of poisoning her former husband. This confession she made, though it exposed her to be burned to death at the stake ; the barbarous punishment then awarded to such an offence, which was regarded as " petty treason."

So great was Mr. Cotton's celebrity as an instructor, that his house was full of young students, some of whom resorted to him from Holland, and some from Germany. In those days, the sons of the Puritans did not repair to the land where too many of the learned, enveloped in the fumes of their unquenchable pipes, " drink beer and think beer," till their brains reek with the noisome smoke of transcendental speculation. The most of Mr. Cotton's pupils were from that University where he had been trained; for Dr. Preston ever counseled his students who had nearly completed the prescribed course of studies, to perfect their preparation for public services by a brief residence with the puritan minister of Boston. It came to be a common saying, that " Mr. Cotton is Dr. Preston's seasoning vessel."

His ministerial labors were abundant. In addition to the ordinary duties of the Sabbath, he preached statedly four times in the week, viz., early each Wednesday and Thursday morning; and again in the afternoons of Thursday and Saturday. Moreover he frequently held other occasional services, in which he often spent six hours in prayer and preaching. When we think of such immense labors sustained through a long course of years, we are at a loss which to admire most; the indefatigable industry of the teacher, or the insatiable eagerness of the people for his instructions. In these degenerate days, such congregations are as rare as such ministers. For several of the latter years of his residence in that well cultured field, he was assisted by a colleague. That was not the era of superabounding periodicals and cheap literature. The mass of the people then depended on hearing, for mental aliment and excitement, as much as now on reading.

Mr. Cotton's usefulness was further extended by a large correspondence with those who sought his aid for resolving obscure points of doctrine, difficult texts of Scripture, or perplexing cases of conscience. Besides this he was considerably occupied every year in providing for the spiritual wants of other congregations; and especially in his native place, where he was held in the highest estimation.

The multiplied toils of this faithful servant were not thrown away. The Spirit of the Lord was with him. There was a surprising reformation of manners in the community. Profaneness was well nigh abolished. Hurtful and superstitious practices were done away. The great body of the people became decidedly religious. As the phrase was, most of the Satanicals had become Puritanicals. The mayor, with the greater part of the magistrates, had embraced the truth. Many scores of devout persons, without forming themselves into a separate church, more fully perfected their existing church-state by solemnly covenanting with God and with each other, to follow the Lord in the purity of his worship. The minister whose fidelity was thus rewarded, was the admiration of his hearers; "exceedingly beloved of the best, and admired and reverenced of the worst." He was held in high respect by some of the chief dignitaries both in Church and State. It was noticed that the temporal prosperity of the town was much promoted by the increased intelligence and good order which pervaded the place in consequence of his activity. On his account it was much resorted to by strangers, and "many gentlemen of good quality" made it their abode.

At this time, Mr. Cotton had a very able colleague, Dr. Anthony Tuckney, afterwards Master of St. John's College, Cambridge. While he filled this latter office, he published a "Briefe Exposition of Ecclesiastes," by Mr. Cotton, a year or two subsequent to the latter's decease. To this volume, printed at London in 1654, Dr. Tuckney prefixed a dedication, addressed to the mayor, with the aldermen and other Christian friends, of Boston, in Lincolnshire. The dedication presents a very happy picture of his joint ministry with Mr. Cotton in that favored place. "The large interest," says Dr. Tuckney, "which I have long enjoyed in your favor, and which you must ever have in my heart, hath emboldened me to prefix your names to this piece; and with the more confidence of its acceptance, because in it an address is made to you at once by *two* who sometimes were together your ministers in the gospel of Christ: by the ever to be honored Mr. Cotton, in the book, and by my unworthy self in the review and dedication of it. Both of us are now removed from you: the one, first to a remote part of the world, there to plant churches,—and thence, after that happy work done, to heaven: the other to some more publique service nearer hand. I often call to mind those most comfortable days, in which I enjoyed the happiness of joint ministry with so able and faithful a guide: and both of us so much satisfaction and encouragement from a people so united in the love both of the truth, and of one another. I cannot read what Paul writeth of his Thessalonians, (in the first chapters of both his epistles to them,) but I think I read over what we then found in Boston. They were then very happy days with you, when your faith did grow exceedingly, and your love to Christ's ordinances, ministers, servants, and to one another abounded. Although your town be situated in a low country, yet God then raised your esteem very high : and your eminency in piety overtopped the height of your steeple. Your name was as an ointment poured out, and your renown went forth for that beauty and comeliness, which God had put upon you."

How can we refrain from lamenting, that a Christian flock, so happily and profitably united under the guidance of its beloved pastors, could not escape the fury of religious tyranny? Such interference is impotent as to any good, but all powerful for evil. There is evidence, that the leaven of Mr. Cotton's piety long lingered in that once favored place. Perhaps we have an evidence that its influence is still, in some measure, transmitted to the present inhabitants. In this year, 1846, the mayor and aldermen of that ancient corporation addressed a letter to the civic authorities of Boston in New England. This well written communication was sent with the noble design of drawing closer the bonds of amity between two countries which were apprehended to be in some danger of coming to hostilities. In this friendly missive, the people of the mother town do not fail to remind the transatlantic daughter, that she is indebted to them of old for their famous Mr. Cotton, and their more famous name. From thence is drawn an argument for the peace of the nations to which these cities respectively belong.

His learning, and his ability in putting it to good use, made him a special favorite with Archbishop Williams. And when that prelate was bishop of Lincoln, and also Lord Keeper of the Great Seal, being the last ecclesiastic who held that office in England, he went to the imperious James I., and made so favorable a report of Mr. Cotton's singular worth and learning, that the king gave consent that his ministry should not be interrupted on account of his non-conformity. And this was very remarkable, when we consider that monarch's impetuosity and exasperation against such as offended in that particular. The mystery of Mr. Cotton's impunity was not known to Samuel Ward, of facetious memory, the author of the "Simple Cobbler." He remarked in his pleasant manner, "Of all men in the world, I envy Mr. Cotton, of Boston, most; for he doth nothing by way of conformity, and yet hath his liberty: and I do almost every thing that way, and cannot enjoy mine."

The vicar of Boston was very much respected by the earls of Dorchester and Lindsay. These noblemen being in the vicinity, attending to the draining of some part of the Lincolnshire fens, came to hear this noted preacher. His text that day was Gal. 2 : 20 ; "I am crucified with Christ," &c. ; and he was prepared to discourse on the duty of living by faith in adversity. But considering that these high and mighty lords had never been very conversant with adversity, he promptly reversed his subject, and expatiated on the duty of living by faith in prosperity. It is said, that they also heard him discourse on civil government, and were greatly captivated with the wisdom and spirit by which he spake. They assured him of their friendship ; and offered, if ever it should be needed, to exert all their influence at the royal court in his behalf. When these puissant nobles had occasioned some scandal by indulging in diversions unsuitable to the Sabbath, they kindly accepted his discreet admonitions, and promised reformation. His faithful dealing is the more to be commended, when we take into account the profound veneration then felt for those who were so favored in the accident of birth. We have heard old countrymen, advanced in years, tell of the awful respect in which nobility was held in their young days : so that in attempting to speak to a peer of the realm with his star upon his breast, the tongue would cleave to the roof of the mouth.* The French revolution seems to have forever broken down this feeling of overpowering veneration for aristocracy. We look upon an anointed king with far less emotion in these times, when reverence for mere rank is rapidly passing away.

Toward the end of his residence in Boston, Mr. Cotton was for a whole year disabled from preaching, by a quartern ague, which began in September, 1630. His physicians advising a change of air, he removed to the mansion of the earl of Lincoln, another of his noble friends, whose Countess was a lady of eminent piety. Among their children was the celebrated lady Arbella Johnson, and also the lady Susan, wife of John Humphrey, one of the assistants. Both of these ladies settled, and the former died, in this colony of Massachusetts. In the hospitable dwelling of their parents, Mr. Cotton recovered his health : but lost his estimable wife by the same disease, after a happy and religious union of eighteen years. About a year after, he mar-

* It is said, that a young lady from the country being ushered into the dread presence of Sarah, Duchess of Marlborough, lost all her self-possession, and falling upon her knees, mechanically recited her customary grace at meals : "Lord, make us suitably thankful for what we are about to receive !"

ried an estimable widow, Mrs. Sarah Story, who was an endeared friend of his former wife. Good Mr. Norton, speaking of these grave and godly matrons, compares them with Euodias and Syntyche, "which labored with Paul in the gospel."

Not long after his second marriage, the tempest, which had been delayed for so many years, broke forth. There was in the town a dissipated character, Gawain Johnson by name, whose irregularities had brought him under the notice of the correctional police. Resolved to be revenged upon the magistrates by whom he had been punished, he went up to London, and filed an information against them in that infamous tribunal, the High Commission Court. This body was styled the "High Commissioners for Causes Ecclesiastical:" and was first set up by Queen Elizabeth in 1559. It was composed of bishops, privy counselors, officers of state, lawyers, deans, and the like, to the number of forty or more; three of whom, usually with a bishop, or other dignitary, at their head, were vested with full power to inquire into and punish all opinions or practices different from those of the established Church. All such cases they could try, either with or without a jury, the whole supremacy and despotism of the monarch being committed into their hands by royal commission. Persons informed against by letter only were cited before them; and in trying them, no regard was had to the statute laws of the realm. The accused were tossed about in the vast, stormy and most uncertain gulf of the common law; where shipwreck was almost inevitable. The most odious of the proceedings in that court, in which witnesses were not openly examined, was the oath *ex officio;*—an oath by which the prisoner was required to answer any question which should be put to him, no matter how deeply the answer might injure him. If he refused to swear, he was severely punished for contempt of court; if he answered, he was convicted on his own confession. This outrage was systematically committed against every principle of law and justice, requiring that no man shall be compelled to criminate himself. Hume has justly denounced the High Commission as a "real Inquisition; attended with similar iniquities and cruelties." * Dr. Lingard, himself a Romanist, says: "The chief difference consisted in their names. One was the court of Inquisition, the other of High Commission." † This tribunal, while it lasted, was in

* Eliz., chap. xli.

† History of England, vol. v., chap. vi.

truth a very efficient substitute for the Inquisition, which Du Plessis Mornay energetically called, "that hell of the papacy."

The charge made at the office of this infamous court against the Boston magistrates, was for not kneeling at the sacrament, and for neglecting some other ceremonies of the like importance. The officers of the court required that the minister's name should be inserted. "Nay," said the informer, Johnson, "the minister is an honest man, and never did me any wrong." But being told that his complaint would be thrown out unless it included the name of the minister who permitted the alledged irregularities, the miserable man, rather than lose his revenge, inserted the name of one who had never injured him. Upon this, letters missive were forthwith despatched to bring Mr. Cotton before that dreaded bar.

The Rev. John Rogers of Dedham, in England, one of the sons of that Marian martyr who used to be figured in the rude wood-cuts of the New England Primer, was informed of the accusation entered against Mr. Cotton. Mr. Rogers received the sorrowful tidings just as he was going to preach his weekly lecture. In his discourse he deeply lamented the occurrence, and broke out, with a sort of prophetic fire, in words to this effect:—"As for that man who hath caused a faithful pastor to be driven from his flock, he is a wisp used by the hand of God for the scouring of his people. But mark the words now spoken by a minister of the Lord! I am verily persuaded, that the judgments of God will overtake the man that hath done this thing; either he will die under a hedge, or something else, more than the ordinary death of men, shall befall him." Those old men of God did not hesitate to venture a prediction of this kind; for they had full often witnessed the wretched end of such characters;

"And old experience doth attain,
To something like prophetic strain."

and it came accordingly to pass, that this sorry informer, very shortly after, died of the plague under a hedge in Yorkshire. Through fear of contagion, he perished alone, and was left long unburied. Our fathers, who were exceedingly inquisitive and trustful in such matters, did not fail to recognize in this event an evident divine retribution from the hand of Him, who, as the Psalmist saith, "hath bent his bow, and made it ready,—who ordaineth his arrows against the persecutors."

Good Mr. Whiting, "the angel of the church in Lynn," where he was the first pastor, was himself a native of old Boston. He wrote a biographical sketch of Mr. Cotton, which was the basis of John Norton's more extended memoir, on which latter work Cotton Mather enlarged considerably. To the facts related in Mather's very valuable account, the present narrative makes very great additions collected from every available source. This Mr. Whiting, speaking of John Cotton's enemies, who secretly plotted, or openly acted, against him in old Boston, remarks:—"They all of them were blasted, either in their names, or in their estates, or in their families, or in their devices, or else came to untimely deaths; which shows how God hath owned his servant in his holy labors; and that in the things wherein they dealt proudly against him, he would be above them." Doubtless, the avenging providence of God is not to be rashly scrutinized. We cannot be too cautious in the interpretation of such matters. And yet a broad induction of facts will justify the solemn conclusion, that "verily there is a God that judgeth in the earth." His people are his charge. "Yea, he hath reproved kings for their sakes; saying, Touch not mine anointed, and do my prophets no harm."

Mr. Cotton, warned that letters missive were issued against him, concealed himself from the eager search of the pursuivants by flight. He was aware that, if apprehended, he had nothing better to expect than to pine in perpetual imprisonment, in which so many of his brethren had worn out their shortened days. During his concealment, his potent friend, the Earl of Dorchester, or as more commonly called, Dorset, who was a thorough courtier, lord chamberlain to the queen, and far enough from being a Puritan, exerted all his influence in the case. But that grinding and remorseless oppressor, Laud, who, about this time, was made archbishop of Canterbury, and who on the very day that he became primate and metropolitan of all England, received, by a significant coincidence, the offer of a cardinal's hat from Rome, was inexorable. That bitter prelate would often exclaim: "O that I could meet with Cotton!" The noble earl, perceiving that all his intercessions must be unavailing, wrote to the irreproachable fugitive, that "if he had been guilty of drunkenness, or uncleanness, or any such *lesser* fault, he could have obtained his pardon; but inasmuch as he had been guilty of non-conformity and puritanism, the crime was unpardonable;" and ended with advising him to fly for his safety. It is not surprising, after this sample of their quality, that Mr. Cotton should long after say:

"The ecclesiastical courts are like the courts of the high priests and pharisees, which Solomon, by a spirit of prophecy stileth, dens of lions and mountains of leopards. And those who have to do with them, have found them markets of the sins of the people, the cages of uncleanness, the forges of extortion, the tabernacles of bribery."

There is extant a letter, dated October 3, 1632, written by Mr. Cotton while under concealment, to the lady he had but lately married. It is here inserted as presenting a confidential expression of his feelings at the time.

Dear &c. If our heavenly Father be pleas'd to make our Yoke more heavy than we did so soon expect, remember I pray thee what we have heard, that our heavenly Husband the Lord Jesus, when he 1st called us to Fellowship with himself, called us unto this Condition, to deny ourselves, and to take up our Cross daily, to follow him. And truly, tho' this Cup be brackish at the first; yet a Cup of God's mingling is doubtless sweet in the Bottom, to such as have learned to make it their greatest Happiness to partake with Christ, as in his Glory, so in the Way that leadeth to it. Where I am for the present, I am very fitly and welcomely accommodated, I thank God : so as I see here I might rest desired enough till my Friends at Home shall direct further. They desire also to see thee here, but that I think it not safe yet, till we see how God will deal with our Neighbours at Home : for if you should now travel this Way, I fear you will be watched and dogged at the Heels. But I hope shortly God will make Way for thy safe Coming. The Lord watch over you all for Good, and reveal himself in the Guidance of all our Affairs. So with my Love to thee, as myself, I rest; desirous of thy Rest and Peace in him. J. C.

This letter, written under such circumstances of painful separation, imminent peril, and uncertainty for the future, betrays no petulant impatience or unmanly repinings. It beautifully portrays the sublime peacefulness of the mind, which, in the hour of adversity, is stayed on God. Within six weeks from the writing of the above letter, this pious couple was again united, though obliged still to live in concealment.

After earnest prayer for divine direction, and much consultation with good men upon the subject, Mr. Cotton concluded to seek refuge in Holland, whither so many of the Puritan ministers and people had already fled from the violence of persecution. Some of his Boston friends urged him to permit them to sustain and protect him, that they might privately enjoy the benefit of his ministry, without which they must be exposed to great temptation. But the venerable Mr. Dod, an old Puritan famous for his piety and his wit, told them, "that the removing of a minister was like the draining of a fish-pond: the good fish will follow the water; but eels, and other refuse fish, will stick in the mud."

That there were in the pond some good fish, with life enough to follow the water, appears from Mr. Cotton's book on the "Holinesse of Church-Members," printed many years after in 1650. It is dedicated "to my honored, worshipful and worthy friends, the Mayor and Justices, the Aldermen and Common Council, together with the whole Congregation and Church at Boston." Speaking of old times with them, he says;—"And ye became followers of us, and of the Lord; and showed yourselves ensamples in some first fruits of reformation, unto many neighbor congregations about you: 1 Thess. 1: 6, 7. And though you saw, that any small measure of reformation, (which then was offensive to the State, and suffered under the name of NON-CONFORMITY,) would expose yourselves to some sufferings, unless you deserted me, yet I bear you record, you chose rather to expose yourselves to charge and hazard for many years together, than to expose my ministry to silence. And though, at last, in that hour and power of darkness, when the late High Commission began to stretch forth their malignant arm against us, I was forced to depart secretly from you, (from some of you, I say,) howbeit, not without the privity and consent of the chief, yet sundry of you yielded up yourselves, as Ittai to David, to follow the Lord whithersoever he should call; and to go along with me, whether to life or death, in this late howling wilderness. And though, after my departure, you were somewhat carried aside with the torrent of the times, yet, I believe, not without some apprehension of the light of the word going before you, in your judgments, to the satisfaction of your own consciences. And ever since that time, wherein the strong hand of the Lord, and the maglignancy of the times, had set this vast distance of place, and great gulf of seas, between us; yet still you claimed an interest in me, and have yearly ministered some real testimony of your love. And at last, when the Lord, of his rich grace, had dispelled the storm of malignant church-government, you invited me again and again, to return unto the place and work wherein I had walked before the Lord and you in former times. But the estate of those of you who came along with me, and who thereby had most interest in me, could not bear that. Nor would my relation to the church here suffer it. Nor would my age, now stricken in years, nor infirm body, ill-brooking the seas, be able to undergo it, without extreme peril of becoming unserviceable either to yourselves or others."

From this document we learn several things, which might not otherwise have come to our knowledge. It appears, that the affections of his old flock clung to their banished minister: and that, through some twenty years of absence, they annually sent him substantial tokens of their anxiety to promote his comfort. We find too, that when the execution of William Laud and Charles Stuart had removed the bar to his return, they sent him such reiterated and urgent calls as could be declined only for the most imperative reasons.

To these reasons there is another to be added. While the Long Parliament was at the height of its power, before Cromwell had dosed it with his "purging colonels," the presbyterial form of government was imposed by law on the parishes of England. Presbyterianism, at that time, admitted persons confessedly unregenerate to the Lord's table. In reference to this, Mr. Cotton told his importunate friends;—"The estate of your church, admitting more than professed saints to the fellowship of the seals, and the government of your church subjected to an extrinsical ecclesiastical power, would have been perpetual scruples and torments to my conscience, which, knowing the terrors of the Lord, and the conviction of my own judgment, I durst not venture upon." To this he adds, in his charitable, unreproaching manner;—"Not that I misjudge others who can satisfy their consciences in a larger latitude: but because every man is to be fully persuaded in his own mind, and I must live by my own faith. Rom. 14: 5."

Mr. Cotton did not lay down his pastoral charge in any summary or informal manner. He first obtained the consent of his people, so far as it was possible to consult them on the subject. "On this point," he says, "I conferred with the chief of our people, and offered them to bear witness to the truth I had preached and practiced amongst them, even unto bonds, if they conceived it might be any confirmation to their faith and patience. But they dissuaded me from that course, and thinking it better for themselves, and for me, and for the Church of God, to withdraw myself from the present storm, and to minister in this country [New England, whence this letter was written] to such of their town as they had sent before hither, and such others as were willing to go along with me, or to follow after me."*

Governor Hutchinson has preserved for us a letter† to Dr. Williams, Bishop of Lincoln, written by Mr. Cotton, a few weeks before sailing for America, for the purpose of resigning his vicarage into the prelate's hands. Dr. Williams had showed him all the indulgence he could, till Laud compelled the reluctant prelate to resort to rigorous measures. Mr. Cotton gratefully acknowledges the diocesan's kindness, gives a short account of the drift of his ministry at Boston, and assigns the reasons of his departure in a manner the most meek and respectful, and yet happily blended with a high principled firmness and religious independence. This communication breathes the deepest solicitude for the welfare of the flock from which he was torn away.

Being thus fully released from all obligation of duty to his recent charge, he took measures

* See letter, dated Dec. 3, 1634, in Hutchinson's Original Papers, page 56.

† Original Papers, p. 249, &c. The letter is dated May 7 : 1633.

to effect his escape from his native shores. To shun the officers who were on the watch for his apprehension, he traveled under an assumed name and a change of garb, toward the port where he expected to embark for Holland. But when he had nearly reached the place, he was met by one of his relatives, who, by dint of persuasion and entreaty, induced him to betake himself to London.

There were then in that city three pious ministers who considered the imposed ceremonies as things in themselves of little consequence, and as such submitted to them. One of these was Dr. Goodwin, a clergyman of great distinction, and afterwards one of the leading divines in the renowned Westminster Assembly. The cynical Anthony Wood styles him and Dr. Owen, "the two Atlasses and Patriarchs of Independency." Another of the three alluded to was Mr. Thomas Nye, in high repute for learning. The other was John Davenport, the founder of the New Haven colony, and one of the "chief fathers" of New England. These gentlemen embraced the opportunity of holding a conference with Mr. Cotton. Knowing him to be an exceedingly dispassionate and judicious man, they made no doubt but that they should convince him, that it was his duty to conform rather than to leave his country and his flock. At this conference he first confuted all the arguments they could array to justify their conformity: and then vindicated his own course in choosing to undergo so great privations, rather than to defile his conscience by acquiescing in customs which derogated from the kingly office of the great Head of the Church. As the result of these discussions, these three able champions came entirely over to Mr. Cotton's views. Nor does this detract at all from their just reputation, but rather enhances it. "For he that is overcome of the truth parteth victory with him that overcometh, and hath the best share for his own part." These men belonged to that class of which good Fuller says, that "they count themselves the greatest conquerors, when the truth hath taken them captive." The three, not long after, themselves became exiles for the truth to which they had honorably yielded.* After Mr. Cotton's death, Mr. Davenport gave a glowing account of this interesting debate, in which, he

* This Dr. Goodwin lay wind-bound, in hourly expectation that the pursuivants would seize him before the wind would favor his escape to Holland. Distressed as he was for a more propitious gale, he cried, "Lord, if thou hast at this time any poor servant of thine who wants this wind more than I do another, I do not ask for the changing of it: I submit unto it. The wind soon came about, and carried him clear from his pursuers.

says, Mr. Cotton "answered with great evidence of Scripture light, composedness of mind, mildness of spirit, constant adhering to his principles, and keeping them unshaken." The trio of friends in this amicable contention were struck with admiration at his might in the Scriptures, his vast and various reading, his prompt memory, his ready reply, and his government of his own spirit, far beyond what they had "taken notice of in any man before him." Mr. Davenport closes by saying;—"The reason of our desire to confer with him rather than any other touching these weighty points, was our former knowledge of his approved godliness, excellent learning, sound judgment, eminent gravity, candor and sweet temper of spirit, whereby he could placidly bear those that differed from him in their apprehensions. All which, and much more we found; and glorified God, in him, and for him." This description explains the secret of Mr. Cotton's uncommon success as a debater, and as a resolver of the doubtful and difficult questions in his casuistry which were constantly submitted to him for solution. Truly, these men who are so firmly tenacious of their opinions, and yet thus maintain them in the spirit of love and the meekness of wisdom, are usually the most invincible and irresistible in debate.

In John Cotton's "Covenant of Grace," a book written long after this, in America, of which several editions were printed, there is, in that of 1655, an Address to the reader, by Rev. Thomas Allen, minister of St. Edward's, Norwich, Eng., who a few years before had been teacher of the church in Charlestown, Mass. The addresser says of the author: "He was a man of peace, of a very sweet spirit, and had a very special faculty of composing differences in the judgments of the brethren. And thus much I shall crave liberty to testify of him, that, besides the multiplicity of occasions which was constantly upon him, he was not without care about the peace and welfare of the churches abroad; and notwithstanding his so vast a distance in body from the churches and saints in his native country, yet he had great thoughts in heart for the division of his brethren here, being seriously studious how to compose and heal their breaches. He hath sometimes said unto me, being privately together;—'Brother, I perceive there is a great *gravamen* which the one party is much offended at with the other. I pray let us study how we may ease and remove it.'"

Mr. Whiting gives him this character as a disputant:—"He was of admirable candor, of unparalleled meekness, of rare wisdom, very loving even to those that differed in judgment from him, yet one that held his own stoutly, tightly maintaining and keenly defending what himself judged to be the truth." Beware of such men, unless you be willing to accord with them.

It is worth mentioning here, that among the auditors in that London conference, was Rev. Henry Whitfield, rector of Oakley in Surrey, who from that time became a conscientious non-conformist, and was afterwards the founder of the town and church of Guilford, in the New Haven colony.

While secreted at London, by Mr. Davenport and other ministers, Mr. Cotton gave up the design of proceeding to Holland. He was discouraged from betaking himself to that country, for the same reasons which induced Mr. Robinson's Leyden flock to leave it for America. Letters from Governor Winthrop, and from the infant church in our own Boston, decided him to shun the fires of persecution by braving the waters of the ocean, then much more formidable to the voyager than now.

It was about the middle of July, 1633, when Mr. Cotton, with Thomas Hooker and Samuel Stone, two ministers of great note, and with a number of his old Boston parishioners, commenced his adventurous voyage. They sailed in a vessel called the Griffin, the name of a fabled creature, partly eagle and partly lion. It was a ship of three hundred tons, having at this time about two hundred passengers, of whom four died while on the way.

Mr. Cotton and Mr. Hooker experienced much difficulty in getting out of England; for long search had been made for them by the emissaries of that odious instrument of all sorts of tyranny, the High Commission Court. All the ports were waylaid for their apprehension; and at the Isle of Wight, where it was expected that the Griffin would have made her last stoppage, she was strictly searched by the pursuivants. But the staunch ship afterwards, by private agreement, lay off the Downs; and, griffin-like, with lion heart and eagle wings, swooped upon the prey, and bore it in triumph from the disappointed hunters.

But oh, the sadness of that hour! when the hapless exiles, relieved at last from the haunting fear of capture, felt all their love of home rise in the strength of that mastering passion. Forgetting the bitterness of their lot, and regardless of the hardships of the future, they wept their last farewell to parted friends, and to the native land they should see no more. Natural affection was strong; but gracious affection was stronger. The love of Christ constrained them. God counted their bitter tears; and they have found them each a pearl in heaven. "And Jesus answered and said, Verily I say unto you, there is no man that hath left house, or brethren, or sisters, or father, or mother, or wife, or children, or lands, for my sake and the gospel's, but he shall receive an hundred-fold now in this time, houses, and brethren and sisters, and mothers, and children, and lands, with persecutions; and in the world to come, eternal life."

We almost envy our fathers for their distressing opportunity of evincing the strength, sincerity and purity of their love to Jesus, before they went to meet him joyfully at his judgment-seat. And is there no way, in which the tenderness and constancy of our love may be put to decisive proof? Can we do nothing to show that our hearts are wholly given to the Lord? Aye, by crucifying our bosom-sins, by pure and holy living, by unremitted efforts for the salvation of men, by our utmost exertions to promote the Church's grand mission work of the world's conversion, by ceaseless sacrifices joyfully made in the holy cause of benevolence,—by these, we too may prove that Jesus has full possession of our souls. Thus may we make it manifest, that, in blood and in spirit, we are the sons of the pilgrims. This shall argue for us, that we are ready, if persecution should arise, to suffer what our fathers endured :—that we are ready to walk, like them, with firm, unfaltering step, through pains and perils for conscience' sake : that we are ready to follow on, through despoilment, exile, bonds and death, to the celestial throne, and the crown eternal.

CHAPTER V.

Voyage to America. Birth of Seaborn Cotton. Arrival at Boston. Small beginnings. Interest felt in Mr. Cotton's coming. Admission to the church. Installation. Laying on of hands, why used. Distinction between the offices of pastor and teacher. Not two orders in the ministry, but different employments of the same order. "God's promise to his Plantations." Mr. Cotton's services in giving form and order to ecclesiastical and civil affairs. Utility of order.

It was about the middle of July, in 1633, when Mr. Cotton commenced his voyage. Both he and Mr. Hooker preserved their disguise, till they were so far over the main ocean, that they could safely disclose who they were. Mr. Stone, who was much the youngest, and for whom the search was not so furious, performed all the public religious duties of the ship's company, till his companions could resume their character as preachers, and officiate in their turns.

This was a richly freighted ship, bearing a large part of the fortune of New England. Our pun-loving ancestors observed, at her coming, that God had supplied them with three necessary commodities: "*Cotton* for their clothing, *Hooker* for their fishing, and *Stone* for their building." During the voyage, they usually had three services every day; which was, perhaps, the first example of a "protracted meeting." When they had been a month at sea, Mr. Cotton, whose first wife died childless, became a father. This, his eldest child, received the name *Seaborn*, in commemoration of the mercies attending his birth. Seaborn Cotton lived to be a highly useful and honored minister of the gospel. There were other children born on the same passage. At the end of seven weeks, which was then regarded as a remarkably expeditious and prosperous voyage, they landed at what is now the good old city of Boston, on the third day of September, 1633.

This place had then been settled three years. Governor Dudley says, that the first settlers, previous to their coming hither, had already determined to name the place they should fix upon after the scene of Mr. Cotton's pastoral labors, and in compliment to him, with the hope that it might be some little inducement to him to come there himself. The compliment, however, at the time, was not so very flattering. For so forlorn and unimposing was this little out-of-the-way settlement, that our fathers, who delighted in puns, anagrams, alliterations, and other modes of playing upon words, used rather familiarly to call it *Lost-town.* Let them be excused, if, by such pleasantries, they sometimes sought to alleviate the discomforts of their lot. The place soon began to wear a more cheering aspect; and flourished more and more, till it far exceeded in importance the parent-town whose name it inherited. Our elder writers ascribe much of its early prosperity to the wisdom, conduct and credit of Mr. Cotton; who seems to have had something of the talent of the Athenian statesman, who, when laughed at because he had no skill to touch the lute, retorted that he knew not how to fiddle; but he knew how to raise a small city into a powerful state. In New England, "a little one became a thousand, a small one a strong nation."

Just before his arrival, the people had been holding a special season of fasting and prayer, urging their covenant with God as a reason why he should send them a spiritual guide, to be unto them, like Hobab to the tribes of Israel, "as eyes in the wilderness." Their supplications were answered in the gift of this "able minister of the New Testament." Mr. Cotton was then about forty-eight years of age, and ripe in wisdom, knowledge, experience and grace. At his coming, his services were called for in different directions. His great capacities for usefulness were considered to be the common property of the whole colony; and it was at first proposed, that his support should be provided for from the colonial treasury, in consideration of the public benefit expected to accrue from his labors. This motion however, was, very properly, overruled. The magistrates and other leading men decided, that this great light must be set in the chief candlestick; and, within a fortnight, designated him to be Teacher of the First Church in Boston, of which the Rev. John Wilson was then Pastor.

Mr. Cotton was first to be admitted to the church. This was an interesting scene. There was a stated religious service held on the Saturday evenings. At the first of these meetings after his landing, he, by request, took part in the discussion of the question, which, on that occasion, happened to be in reference to the church. He expatiated upon the diversities in the spiritual state and grades of purity of different churches. He showed from the Song of Solomon 6: 8, that some churches are as queens, some as concubines, and some as virgins. After this, he and his wife were propounded for admission.

On the Lord's day following, he conducted the exercises of public worship in the afternoon. He then expressed his desire to make a confession of his faith, according to usage. His confession related chiefly to the subject of baptism, which he then desired for his child. He gave his reasons for not baptizing it while at sea; from which it appears, that he then held that the sacraments can only be administered in a settled congregation, or organized church; and also, that a minister, notwithstanding his official character, can dispense the seals only in his own congregation. On this last point, at least, he afterwards changed his views so far as to maintain that a minister might give the sacraments in a church which is destitute of the proper officers.

Mr. Cotton next requested the admission of his wife, to whose qualifications for membership he bore "a modest testimony." He craved that she might be excused from making a public oral profession of her faith, as was then the custom of the church. He regarded the practice as 'unfit for women's modesty," and contrary to the apostle's rule. To her examination in private by the elders, he had no objections. So she was asked, whether she consented to the confession of faith made by her husband, and concurred in his desire for admission. Upon her answering in the affirmative, they were both admitted by vote of the church. Their child was then baptized by Mr. Wilson, the father himself presenting it. At the baptism of another child, which took place at the same time, he gave it as a reason for disusing the unscriptural and unnatural custom of employing sponsors, that the ordinance was designed as the "parents' *incentive* for the help of their faith."

A month afterwards, October 10, 1633, a day of fasting was observed. Thomas Leverett, "an ancient, sincere professor," an old parishioner of Mr. Cotton, and his fellow-voyager to this country, was chosen ruling elder; and Mr. Firmin, "a godly man," was elected deacon. These officers were ordained by imposition of the hands of the presbytery: that is to say, the pastor, and such ruling elders as were previously in office. The pastor and other officers of each particular church constituted the presbytery of that church; and in this sense alone can the term *Presbyterian* apply to our Congregational Churches.

This business being over, Mr. Cotton was then publicly chosen by the Church to be their Teacher, which was made manifest by the members' lifting up their hands. Next, the pastor, Wilson, demanded of him whether he accepted that call. After a pause, he replied to the effect, that he knew his unworthiness and insufficiency for the place ; yet, recounting the particular passages of God's providence which concurred to call him to it, he felt himself constrained in duty to accept it. Upon this, the pastor and two ruling elders laid their hands upon his head, and the pastor prayed. Then, removing their hands, they again placed them on his head ; and calling him by name, from thenceforth separated him to the said office in the name of the Holy Ghost, laid upon him the charge of the congregation, and in this significant manner indued him with all the privileges of his station. Last of all, they formally blessed him. The presbytery of the church having thus completed its part in this interesting ceremony, the ministers of the neighboring churches there present gave him, at the pastor's request, the right hand of fellowship. The pastor finally made a mutual stipulation between the church and its newly inducted teacher.

In respect to the solemn imposition of hands, just spoken of, or ordination as it is often termed, we must observe that it does not follow of course, that Mr. Cotton renounced the ministry he had formerly received in the Church of England.

This may seem to be the natural supposition. But it must be borne in mind, that when, three years before, Mr. Wilson was constituted teacher of the same church, it was done in a similar manner; but with a protestando, that it was no reordination, as we now understand the term. These are the words of Governor Winthrop, who assisted on that occasion: "We used imposition of hands, *but with this protestation by all*, that it was only as a sign of election and confirmation, not of any intent that Mr. Wilson should renounce his ministry he received in England." * This is sufficiently explicit. And when the same Mr. Wilson, about one year prior to Mr. Cotton's arrival, was made pastor of the same church in which he had been thus constituted teacher, this too was done by the laying on of the hands of the ruling elder and the deacons. Of course, in this case, no protestation was needed, for it is impossible to suppose that the Church would nullify its own previous ordinance. Nor was any express protestation necessary in Mr. Cotton's case; for it had already been established, by the precedent in Mr. Wilson's instance, that no renunciation of his previous ministerial authority was intended.

* Winthrop's History of New England, vol. 1, p. 32, 33, Savage's edition.

The first installation in New England in which the laying on of hands was omitted, was that of Rev. Charles Morton, settled over the First Church in Charlestown, the 5th of November, 1686. Mr. Morton thus alludes to the subject in a letter written some three years after to the right honorable Hugh Boscawen, Esq., in England: "Though their custom has been a new imposition of hands upon every new call to the exercise of the ministry, yet to us, who came from Europe, Mr. Bailey* and myself, it was abated. And for aught I can perceive, they mind more the *substance* of religion, than the *circumstances* of some men's private opinions." † Dr. Increase Mather gave the charge, "and spoke in praise of the Congregational way, and said, Were he as Mr. Morton, he would have hands laid on him." Rev. Joshua Moodey ‡ also, in his prayer, alluded to the subject, and intimated, that "that which would have been grateful to many, namely, laying on of hands, was omitted." § From that time, the precedent

* Installed October 6, 1686, in Watertown, Mass.; afterwards pastor of the First Church in Boston.

† This letter is transcribed in part into a very admirable work by Samuel Mather, D. D., called "An Apology for the Liberties of the Churches in New England." Boston, 1738, p. 148.

‡ Pastor of the First Church in Boston.

§ Budington's History of the First Church in Charlestown, p. 102, 103.

set by Mr. Morton, in the case of resettling ministers who had been previously ordained, was followed more and more, till it became the constant practice. Previous to this change, ministers, in the intervals between one pastoral care and another, were regarded as they are now. They were spoken of, and treated as ministers, and exercised their function as occasion required. Reimposition, when used, was not intended to restore the ministerial character, as though that had been lost; but to designate the person to a special charge.

Our fathers neither regarded imposition of hands as an act that could not be repeated, nor as essential to the validity of an ordination. Theodore Beza, Calvin's famous successor at Geneva, never received it; and, under John Knox's influence, it was for some time disused in Scotland. It was not an act that could not be repeated. They viewed it simply as a solemn designation of the individual to a particular office or duty in the church, and as a sign of investiture. They held, that every true minister must, in the first place, be inwardly called to the work by the Spirit of God, as Aaron was; and then he must be outwardly called by some church of Christ. They held that this power of external vocation, which belongs to the church, is far superior to ordination, which, indeed, is included in it, as the less is included in the greater. The church being able to give a lawful calling to a minister, is much more able to carry that call into effect by the simple ceremony used for that purpose by the brethren in the apostles' time. Hence they maintained the validity of what is sometimes called lay-ordination ; but which they, regarding it as the act of the whole body of the church, the original source of all spiritual power, considered as having in it more of ecclesiastical authority than if performed only by some of its officers acting by delegated powers. Accordingly, in some very few instances, the ceremony was performed, even in the presence of numerous ministers, only by the presbytery, or officers of the particular church, occasionally assisted by some of the brethren. This was done merely by way of asserting and establishing the great principle, that the power of ordination resides in, and emanates from, the Church. After this had been sufficiently understood, it became the invariable custom, and so continues to this day, that the ceremony should be performed by other ministers. But though administered by councils, it is still regarded as done solely at the request of the church which convenes the council for that purpose.

The distinction between the duties of the pastor and teacher, is thus defined in the Cambridge Platform: "The pastor's special work is, to attend to exhortation, and therein to administer a word of wisdom; the teacher is to attend to doctrine, and therein to administer a word of knowledge." Both are empowered to dispense the sacraments, to execute church-censures, and to preach the Word, as to which duties, "they are alike charged withal."* The pastor, on whom chiefly devolved the care of the flock when out of the pulpit, was expected to spend his strength mostly in exhortation, persuading and rousing the church to a wise diligence in the Christian calling. The teacher was to indoctrinate the church, and labor to increase the amount of religious knowledge. His workshop was the study; while the pastor toiled in the open field. Thus Mr. Cotton gave himself up to reading and preparation for the instruction of his people. Twelve hours of close application he used to call "a student's day;" and such a day's work he usually performed, secluded among his books. For intelli-

* Chap. VI., sec. 5.

gence respecting the state of his flock, he depended mostly upon the pastor and ruling elders. He received many visits, but seldom made any himself. Perhaps it may help to a clearer understanding of the difference in the nature of these two offices, to state, that when a case of excommunication occurred, it belonged to the pastor to conduct the business and pronounce the sentence, if the offence related to immorality or "disorderly walking;" but if it were a matter of heretical or erroneous opinions, it was expected that the teacher would preside.

In the estimation of our fathers, the pastor's station was considered to have rather the priority in importance and dignity. It has been a source of perplexity with some, how this could be, seeing that the teacher was sometimes much more distinguished, as to his attainments and general character, than his colleague; as happened in this case of Mr. Cotton as compared with Mr. Wilson. But it seems to be very intelligible, that a man may be pre-eminently endowed with the qualifications needful in a religious teacher, and yet be comparatively unfit for the more active duties of the parochial care. On the other hand, a man may be admirably fitted to *watch* as a pastor over the flock of God, who is comparatively disqualified to *feed* that flock with knowledge and understanding.

It must not be supposed, that our fathers instituted two orders in the ministry. They firmly held, that all ordained ministers were of equal rank; and that there is not the slightest superiority of one over another, except such as results from superior wisdom, knowledge, piety, zeal, and reputation arising from either or all of these, by which individuals are occasionally elevated to a higher degree of estimation and influence than their brethren generally. With them, the terms elder, pastor and bishop, were synonymous and interchangeable, as they are in the New Testament, where they are used as different names for the same office. The distinction between the duties of the pastor and teacher was merely a division of the labors belonging to their common calling; each taking the part for which he was best qualified, without considering whether, in personal matters, he were the greater or more honored of the two. The precedence was accorded to the pastor, because the part of the work assigned to him is essentially the more important part. For "the word of wisdom," in which he was to deal, must be considered as more honorable than "the word of knowledge," which was the allotted province of the other.

Without any disparagement of the latter, we may assent to the poet's estimate of the relative value of each :—

> "Knowledge dwells
> In heads replete with thoughts of other men;
> Wisdom in minds attentive to their own.
> Knowledge, a rude, unprofitable mass,
> The mere materials with which wisdom builds,
> Till smoothed, and squared, and fitted to his place,—
> Does but encumber what it seems to enrich.
> Knowledge is proud, that he has learned so much;
> Wisdom is humble, that he knows no more."

In this matter we may give more weight to an opinion of Martin Luther's, recorded in his "Table Discourses," as it seems in some sort to be a decision against himself. "One asked Luther, Which were greater and better—to strive against the adversaries, or to admonish and lift up the weak? He answered and said, 'Both are very good and necessary; but it is somewhat greater and better to comfort the faint-hearted.'"

The usage which now prevails in our churches does not so much set aside the distinction between pastoral and teaching duties, as blend both offices in one person, who is both pastor and teacher to his congregation. Most of our churches think themselves too small to require the labors of two officers, and too poor to sustain them. It were well, if they generally took better care of the single minister in whom these duties are united. Indeed these duties naturally run into each other, and it is impossible precisely to point out their bound-marks. It is now expected that doctrine shall be preached practically, and that practice be preached doctrinally. It is expected that each shall be so discussed, as that one shall involve the other, and their mutual relations be distinctly exhibited.

Perhaps it would be well for larger and more affluent churches to restore the ancient usage, which our earlier churches practiced so far as they were able. It is very rare to find a person who combines the requisites of a pastor and a teacher in a high and equal degree. And the killing attempt to unite each sort of excellence, where nature had conferred but one, has often occasioned a lamented waste of life and talents. The distinction recognized by our fathers still exists, as it must in the nature of things. How often it is said, Such an one is a fine preacher, but no pastor; and that another is a faithful and successful pastor, but does not excel so much in the pulpit. And their respective hearers, who have sense enough to know that they cannot have every kind of perfection in one man, try to be thankful for such as they have.

About this time Mr. Cotton preached a sermon, which has been repeatedly printed under the title, "God's Promise to his Plantations." Its object is to exhibit the reasons which may justify so serious a step as the forming of a new settlement, like that in which he and his associates were engaged. Its chief felicity, however, is the text, "Moreover I will appoint a place for my people Israel, and I will plant them, that they may dwell in a place of their own, and move no more."* Whatever fastidious critics may think of our forefathers' antiquated sermons, it cannot be denied that they had a singularly happy faculty of finding appropriate texts for every occasion. Mr. Cotton's selection, in the instance now referred to, had the additional merit of being fulfilled in the result. In our fathers and their posterity, was fulfilled that which was spoken by the prophet of the Lord: "He hath cast the lot for them, and his hand hath divided it unto them by line; they shall possess it forever, from generation to generation shall they dwell therein. The wilderness and the solitary place shall be glad for

* 2 Sam. 7: 10.

them; and the desert shall rejoice, and blossom as the rose. It shall blossom abundantly and rejoice, even with joy and singing."

At the time of Mr. Cotton's arrival, the ecclesiastical and civil affairs of the colony were in a confused plight. Under his advice, the state of affairs improved so rapidly, and became so well arranged, as to give some countenance to the expression of one by no means friendly to what he calls "the innovating genius of the great Cotton," and who speaks of him as "sovereign in his dogmas, and absolute in power." One of our oldest historians has said, "Such was the authority he had in the hearts of the people, that whatever he delivered in the pulpit was soon put into an order of court, if of a civil, or set up as a practice in the church, if of an ecclesiastical concernment." *

Our Congregational churches are greatly indebted to him for that pre-eminent liberty they enjoy. The liberty and power which Christ, the King, had vested in his people, had for ages been wrested away by men who, like all usurpers, proved to be tyrants; and turned, as the Puritans said, "the Lord's house into a house of Lords," where they domineered over the

* Hubbard's History of New England.

faith and consciences of the disciples. The rightful power and freedom of the churches was, by Mr. Cotton, deduced afresh from the Scriptures, and fully re-established in practice. Our churches have ever since been nobly jealous and tenacious of that *free ecclesiastical order* which Christ conferred upon them, and for whose restoration they are indebted, under God, to Mr. Cotton and his pious and learned associates.

An eccentric preacher of the Wesleyan persuasion, who has been for some time deceased, is said to have publicly characterized the most numerous denominations in New England in this manner : " The watchword of the Congregationalists is, Order ! order ! That of the Baptists is, Water ! water ! And that of the Methodists is, Fire ! fire ! " We have good reason to be satisfied with our part of this description. For water and fire are good servants, but very bad masters ; or, as the Duke of Bridgewater was wont to say, " They are the best of friends, but the worst of enemies." On the other hand, " order is heaven's first law." It is this which makes all the difference between the stately walls of the temple, and heaps of stones and building lumber. Ben Johnson sententiously observes : " It is only the disease of the unskillful, to think rude things greater than polished, or scattered more numerous than composed." And Dryden's rhyme affords us a valuable precept :—

> " Set all things in their own peculiar place ;
> And know that order is the greatest grace."

Richard Hooker rejoiced, on his death-bed, at the prospect of soon entering a world of order. And doubtless the church on earth will more closely resemble the church in heaven, when every minister and every member shall be, as godly John Norton says Mr. Cotton was, " like the heavenly bodies, always in motion ; but still careful to keep within his proper sphere." The God whom we worship and serve, " is not the author of confusion, but of peace, as in all churches of the saints."

CHAPTER VI.

Principles of Congregational Church Polity. Nature of the Church. Simplicity of worship instituted by the New Testament. Early innovations and perversions. Reformation in England incomplete. Diversities among the Puritans, some at either extreme. Massachusetts Colonists shunned extremes. John Cotton's 'Keys of the Kingdom of Heaven.' Cambridge Platform, 1648. Subject proposed and divided. I. Nature of the Church and its privileges Origin of the name 'Congregational.' Letter to Skelton. Primitive Churches were parochial and independent. Primitive order restored in New England. The Church a monarchy democratically administered. Connection and communion of independent Churches. Dr. Heylin. Cotton's objections to the term 'Independency.' Opposition of Congregationalists to 'Brownism.' Cotton's reply to Baillie. John Robinson's advice. Thomas Shepard. True idea of Church unity. II. Nature and powers of the ministry. Officers of two sorts. The first order. Cotton's view. The second order, or deacons. Apostolical succession discussed. Bishop Hoadley. Archb. Whately. Bishop of Hereford. Macaulay. Ordination, what it is. Archbishop Cranmer. Bishop Burnet. Luther. Popular election of officers. Effect of ordination. Our forefathers free from the hierarchal temper. III. Nature and forms of public worship. What is prayer. Unlawful to *impose* forms. Origin of liturgies. Lord Say and Seal. Origin of English liturgy. Rejected by our fathers. Inconveniences of it. The use of sacraments. Our fathers' discipline commended.

A CHAPTER or two will here be given to an account of the principles and merits of the system of church government instituted by Mr. Cotton and his associates in New England. *Their* views and practices will be presented, avoiding, as far as may be, all controverting of the opinions of others.

The Church, as they viewed it, is the living temple of God. The precious material, wherewith it is constructed, is hewn from the quarry of human nature. The massive blocks had there lain shapeless and senseless, and altogether dead in trespasses and sins. But the Holy Ghost, acting by means of the fire and hammer of God's Word, hath separated them from the formless and lifeless mass, and hath squared and fitted them for their respective places, and hath entered into them and quickened them with an everlasting life, and hath joined them in vital union to Christ, that living Rock of salvation, that head-stone of the corner, that eternal foundation-ledge of Zion. Thus they, "as lively stones, are built up a spiritual house," for "spiritual sacrifices, acceptable to God by Jesus Christ."

The grand temple at Jerusalem, which, allowing for difference of material, was modeled after the plan of the tabernacle of Moses, was intended to serve "unto the example and shadow of heavenly things." It was a type of the celestial or spiritual sanctuary, "of the true tabernacle, which the Lord pitched, and not man." Hence the care with which it was constructed to accord precisely with a prescribed model, "as Moses was admonished of God when he was about to make the tabernacle; for, See, saith he, that thou make all things according to the pattern showed to thee in the mount." The idea of the worldly sanctuary is wholly taken from the heavenly sanctuary.

The instituted worship of God under the older Testament, abounded in forms and ceremonies which had all of them a moral significance embodying some divine truth, or shadowing out some celestial reality. But even that ritual must have nothing of human origin superadded. The Pharisees brought in many innovations derived by tradition of the elders. But Jesus repeats, with approbation, the sentence of the prophet against them:—"In vain do they worship me, teaching for doctrines the commandments of men." Mark the contrast here;—human traditions can never constitute a worship acceptable to God. Therefore God required that his altar should be built only of unhewn stones; and declared that whosoever lifted up a tool upon it had polluted it. The purity of divine worship is defiled by every admixture of man's inventions and devices.

The instituted worship of the New Testament, delights not in figurative pomps and shows, but in plain and literal truth. Its ordinances are few and simple, because it rejoices, not in the "shadows of good things to come," but in the "very image of the things" themselves. Here too, we are to see, that all things be made according to the divine pattern, and kept free from men's contrivances and traditionary enlargements. The worship of the church is to be fashioned after the New Testament exemplar. We have there a fair transcript of the pattern in the mount, a true copy of the ground plan and elevations. To follow this, will be unquestionably safe. To depart from it, will be certainly to go wrong. It is not enough to justify such a usage in divine worship, to say that there is nothing in the Bible expressly against it. "The truth is," as John Norton tersely says, "there is enough against it, if there be nothing for it."

The apostles, "as wise master-builders," left a fabric of doric strength and simplicity. But the fair edifice soon began to be weakened and marred by tasteless changes. And the spiritual architects of the middle ages made sad havoc of the venerable pile. Much of it was rased to the very foundation: and what was built instead, bore the marks of a modern and a meaner style.

The work went on, till the straggling structure presented a strange mixture of the handiwork of different ages and nations. Some remains of the primitive vastness and simplicity were still visible: but oddly blended with Gothic pillars, and Saxon arches, and Norman windows, and Romanesque towers. Most of what was left of the original building was covered up by cumbrous and uncouth additions, and rudely daubed with untempered mortar, or finely plastered over with Italian stucco.

In the first times of the Protestant reformation, much was done toward removing the huge mass of innovations, and restoring the more ancient order. But in England, the work of restitution stopped all too soon. The reformation of doctrine was gloriously effected: but the reformation of order and worship fell far short of recovering the primitive purity. The Puritans felt that the work must go on much farther, before the just and necessary authority of Christ could be re-established in his kingdom. They came at once to the right principle, that the Bible is our only safe and sufficient guide in ecclesiastical practice, as well as in articles of belief.

When our fathers reached these shores, they had a general idea of the nature of that instituted worship which they proposed to set up in conformity with the usage of the primitive Church, in accordance with the pattern in the mount. The details of the plan they had not as yet had opportunity to study, nor had they come to an entire agreement. They were fully determined that every thing should be arranged by the rule of Scripture: but they found some difficulty in the application of this rule, till experience and practice imparted the requisite skill.

There was much diversity of sentiment among the Puritans. Some there were who still conformed, though very discontentedly, with what they felt to be abuses, but which they hoped to see purged away by the Church herself. There were others who conformed in all points, except some two or three. Others still refused conformity in half a dozen points; and others again, as many more. Some went so far as to separate entirely from the Church of England, wholly disowning it as a true Church of God.

The Puritans who formed the Massachusetts colony shunned either extreme. On the one hand, they refused to conform to the abuses which were retained in the mother church: and on the other hand, they resolutely protested, on innumerable occasions, that they were no separatists, and that they were in full communion with all that was right and true in the Churches of England, or any other country. Though, at first, there was considerable diversity of sentiment on minor points among themselves, they, as the light of truth shone progressively brighter, came to an increasing agreement of views. Their practices, at first, from necessity, somewhat uncertain, were modified by degrees, as their experience and their knowledge of the Scripture teachings on the subject became enlarged. But they soon settled down into the usages which have so long been maintained in our churches.

Their first printed guide in ecclesiastical matters was John Cotton's celebrated book, entitled, "The Keyes of the Kingdom of Heaven." This work has been recently republished by one of our enterprising booksellers; and a treatise so curious and instructive ought to have a wide circulation. It is chiefly interesting as a demonstration, that every individual church, with its own officers, is the depository of "the power of the keys." In other words, all the ecclesiastical rights and powers which Christ has given to his Church, are given to every regularly constituted independent church.

In describing the metes and bounds of church power, Mr. Cotton argues that, as in the State, there is a division of powers into several hands, which are to concur in all acts of common concern, and which arrangement results in a healthy constitution of the body politic. This book maintains, that a church, duly organized with its own proper officers, has within itself all that is necessary to its continuance and well-being, and to the management of its own elections, admissions, and censures. Elders and brethren are the constituent members of this sacred corporation. The elders are entrusted with government, the brethren are invested with privilege. The church is so to be ruled by its elders who are over it in the Lord, that without them nothing may ordinarily be done, and that they may have a negative upon the votes of the fraternity, and that they alone may authoritatively preach and administer sacraments:—yet are the brethren to be so upheld in their liberties, that, *unless with their consent*, nothing of common concern may be imposed upon them. Because particular churches may abuse their power, the book of the keys asserts the need of church communion in synods or councils, which may determine, declare or enjoin such things as will correct abuses or disorders in the offending congregations. But still to such churches themselves must be left the *formal acts* which are requisite for carrying out the advice of the council. If such advice should be scandalously and obstinately refused, then it will be the duty of the council to *withdraw communion* from the contumacious church.

This is a summary of the main positions of that once celebrated book; and these positions are sustained by the Cambridge Platform, except what relates to the claim of a veto-power in the elders; on which Mr. Cotton soon ceased to insist.

Soon after its publication, the famous Dr. Owen undertook to confute it; instead of which, quite contrary to his expectation, it confuted and converted him. While speaking of its effect upon his mind, he makes the following remark: "And, indeed, this way of impartial examining all things by the Word, comparing causes with causes, and things with things, laying aside all prejudicate respects unto persons, or present traditions, is a course that I would admonish all to beware of, who would avoid the danger of being made Independents." *

The "Keys of the Kingdom of Heaven," was the standard book of New England church discipline, till the Cambridge Platform was brought

* A Review of the true nature of schism. By John Owen, D. D., chapter II.

forth in 1648, by a synod which sublimely closed its proceedings with singing "the song of Moses and the Lamb," in the fifteenth chapter of the Revelation.

Since the Cambridge Platform was adopted, the custom of our churches has varied in a few particulars from what is recommended there. Thus the Platform advises that each church should have its pastor, its teacher, and its ruling elder, as well as its deacons. And this arrangement, for a while, was generally kept up. But before long, the offices of pastor and teacher were merged in one: or rather, one person filled them both: and the duties of the ruling elder, which principally related to discipline, were practically devolved in the smaller churches upon the pastor and deacons; and in the larger churches, upon a committee chosen for such purposes.

It is not my object to give a complete description of all the usages of Congregationalism at the present day. To do this, with the grounds and reasons of those usages, would require a volume by itself. Nor is it necessary. Every one who wishes to examine the matter, may find all that is important in some of the older and of the more recent publications, where all the information necessary has been laboriously collected, and arranged with admirable judgment and care.

All that will now be attempted, is a general description of the leading features of the church government adopted by the venerated fathers of New England.

This will be presented under three sections.

First, the nature of the church and its privileges;

Secondly, the nature and powers of the ministerial office;

Thirdly, the nature and forms of public worship.

SECTION I.

THE NATURE OF THE CHURCH AND ITS PRIVILEGES.

The term "Congregational" appears to have been first brought into use by John Cotton. His preference for it was grounded on the fact, that the word which, in our English version of the Bible, is rendered *church*, simply and properly means a *congregation*. The word would have been rendered "congregation," if King James had not required his translators to use the word "church" instead. The right sense is given in the nineteenth Article of Religion of the Church of England, where the church is defined to be "a congregation of faithful men, in which the true Word of God is preached, and the sacraments duly administered according to Christ's ordinances, in all those things that of necessity are requisite to the same." So exactly does this language express the Puritan sentiments on the subject, as to justify the celebrated Earl of Shaftesbury, when he said in debate before the house of lords, that he "found the nineteenth article did define the church directly as the Independents do."

In a letter addressed to Rev. Samuel Skelton of Salem by Mr. Cotton, three years before he left England, there is given the following definition of a church:—"It is a flock of saints, called by God into the fellowship of Christ, meeting together in one place, to call upon the name of the Lord, and to edify themselves in communicating spiritual gifts, and partaking of the ordinances of the Lord." After his coming to this country, Mr. Cotton would have added to the above definition, that a mutual *covenant*, express or implied, to unite for the purposes specified, is necessary to complete the constitution of a church. He subscribed to the Cambridge Platform, which teaches, that in the larger and more general sense, "the Catholic church is the whole company of those that are elected, redeemed, and in time effectually called from sin and death unto a state of grace and salvation by Jesus Christ." * In the common and more special sense, the true visible church is "a company of saints by calling, united into one body, by a holy covenant, for the public worship of God, and the mutual edification one of another, in the fellowship of the Lord Jesus." †

The national churches imagine that all the christian people residing in any country form such a congregation. But our fathers held, that the term denotes a literal congregation, meeting statedly in one place for divine worship and ordinances, and united for that purpose into one body by a holy covenant. They could find no trace of any hierarchy in the New Testament. All the acts of church government, and discipline mentioned in that book, were administered by individual churches. They saw, that, in the apostles' time, no one church claimed any right to rule over another. They saw, that each church, great or small, had as full power to manage its own affairs, as though it had been the only church in existence. They saw, that

* Chap. II. sec. 1. † Ib. sec. 5.

each individual church was a complete body of itself, endowed with all the organs of independent vitality, and enabled to do whatever may be needful for its own preservation, well-being, and enlargement.

There is something noble and liberal in this idea, which presents all Christian congregations as so many free, spiritual communities; not governed by others, but each governing itself by he rules and requirements of God's Word. It was only by a long series of usurpations and gradual encroachments, that the churches lost this original and free constitution, and became massed together under the ghostly tyranny of lordly hierarchs.

Our fathers restored in New England the primitive apostolical order by which each several congregation, or church in the ordinary New Testament sense, is divinely empowered to carry on a system of self-government in strict observance of the rules of the gospel, as to election of officers, admission and discipline of members, and general management of its own ecclesiastical affairs. Each church, duly constituted, with its own officers, was entitled to act for itself in all such matters, free from the control of any man, or body of men, external to itself. In the New Testament, our fathers could find no warrant for synodical, or diocesan, or provincial, or national, or parliamentary churches; or for churches organized by civil authority. They found the apostles planting no churches, but such as were parochial: that is to say, distinct congregations, composed of persons possessing the faith, usually meeting in one assembly, and transacting their own business without any subjection to foreign authority. They held, that any organized congregation of believers, formed and kept up under the influences of the Holy Spirit, and the regulations of the written Word of God, is an evangelical church. The view which our fathers took of such a church was this;—It is an absolute monarchy democratically administered. It is an absolute monarchy: for Christ is its supreme Head and King; his will is law; he alone has the right to legislate; and his decrees recorded in the Bible must alone be obeyed. And the affairs of this spiritual monarchy are democratically administered: for to the church is given the free election of all executive officers, and the members are all possessed of equal rights and privileges. What noble schools of liberty and independence of soul, willingly obedient to Christ, but free from vassalage to man, must be found in these self-governing societies!

There is a passage in a letter from Mr. Cotton

to the Lord viscount Say and Seal, which has been supposed to militate against these views. It is in the following words ;—" Democracy I do not conceive that ever God did ordain as a fit government, either for church or commonwealth. If the people be governors, who shall be governed? As for monarchy and aristocracy, they are both of them clearly approved and directed in Scripture, yet so as referreth the sovereignty to himself, [i. e. to God,] and setteth up Theocracy in both, as the best form of government in the commonwealth as well as in the church." * At the first view, this passage seems to be in violent opposition to Mr. Cotton's advocacy of popular institutions on all other occasions. Some, who are friendly to his memory, know not what to make of it; and others regard it as a lure to tempt certain Puritan peers and other great men to come over and join the colonies, as many of them were then thinking to do.

The matter is easily set right by considering the meaning of the words "democracy" and "aristocracy," as used in this letter. The aristocracy spoken of here is elective, and for the most part temporary. Every representative government is an aristocracy, elected by the people to make and

* See the letter in Hutchinson's History of Massachusetts, vol. I., p. 437, &c.

administer the laws, for longer or shorter periods. A simple democracy, according to the primary sense of the word, and the definitions of the ablest political writers, is a state of things in which the whole collected people make and execute the laws. This is mere mob-law, which is no government at all, having neither settled constitution nor executive officers. It is in this sense, that John Cotton denounces democracy; as every reasonable man must do. But the word in our day is taken in a much better sense than formerly, and is used to designate that republican form of government in which the people act through regularly constituted officers of their own choosing. That this was Mr. Cotton's meaning is plain from another passage in the same letter, toward the close, which is quoted for the sake of making him, as he has a right to be, his own interpreter. "Bodine confesseth, that, though it be *status popularis* where the people choose their own governors, yet the government is not a democracy, if it be administered, not by the people, but by the governors, whether one, (for then it is a monarchy, though elective,) or by many, for then, as you know, it is aristocracy. In which respect it is, that church government is justly denied, even by Mr. Robinson, to be democratical, though the people choose their own officers and rulers."* We find the same idea expressed by Mr. Stone of Hartford, when asked to describe the Congregational government. He replied in his scholastic way;—"It is a speaking Aristocracy in the face of a silent Democracy." The church is taught and ruled by officers, who are freely chosen by the people to act in their offices as the Bible directs. This arrangement secures, at once, the order and the liberty of the churches.

Because churches are thus emancipated from all foreign jurisdiction, it must not be supposed, that they are isolated, disconnected bodies, having no mutual relations of love and duty. No: they are a sisterhood: and though all the sisters stand on terms of equality and liberty, they are both necessarily and willingly bound in family ties, the strongest and sweetest of any. As the liberty of the individual Christian is not inconsistent with "the communion of saints," so neither is the liberty of particular congregations inconsistent with the communion of churches. Dr. Heylin, though a bitter hater of the Puritans, has very happily described John Robinson's "model of church government" as "consisting of a coördination of several churches for their mu-

* Hutchinson's Hist. I., 439.

tual comfort; not a subordination of the one to the other, in the way of direction or command. Hence," he adds, "came the name of 'Independents,' continued unto those amongst us who neither associate themselves with the Presbyterians, nor embrace the frenzies of the Anabaptists." It is mostly by this name of "Independents" that the Congregationalists, who are now so numerous in England, are generally known in that country. That name, however, was not wholly satisfactory to Mr. Cotton. He remarks upon it as follows:—"Nor is 'Independency' a fit name for the way of our churches: for in some respects it is too strait, and in others too large. It is too strait, in that it confineth us within ourselves, and holdeth us forth as independent of all others: whereas indeed we do profess dependence upon magistrates for civil government and protection, dependence upon Christ and his Word for the sovereign government and rule of our administrations, dependence upon the counsel of other churches and synods when our own variance or ignorance may stand in need of such help from them; and therefore this title of 'Independency' straiteneth us and restraineth us from our necessary duty and due liberty. Again, in other respects, 'Independency' stretcheth itself too largely and more generally than that it can single out us, for it is compatible to a national church as well as to a congregational.—Wherefore, if there must needs be some note of difference to decypher our estate and to distinguish our way, I know of none fitter than to denominate ours—'Congregational.'" * The name 'Independent' is expressly disapproved by the Cambridge Platform.†

Some of the more rigid Separatists, known by the uncouth title of Brownists, carried the idea of independency to such an extreme as to render every church an isolated body, dwelling solitarily, without a sisterhood, and the cheering interchange of acts of communion. They were hurried to this extremity, by the excessive anxiety to avoid any entanglement which might again ensnare them in the meshes of ecclesiastical bondage. Mr. Cotton and his coadjutors happily avoided a sentiment so destructive of all the benefits of the fellowship of the churches. In replying to Baillie, Mr. Cotton takes occasion to say of Brown;—"Neither in whole nor in part do we partake in his schism; he separated from churches and from saints; we, only from the world, and from that which is of the world."—"Though we put not such honor upon those

* Way of Congregational Churches Cleared, p. 11.

† Chap. II. Sect. 5.

he calls 'Brownists,' as to own them for our 'fathers,' yet neither do we put so much dishonor upon them as to 'heap coals of contumely' upon their heads: we look not on them with contempt, but compassion."* Mr. Cotton concurred in sentiment with the excellent John Robinson, who, in his parting instructions to that part of his flock which was about to proceed from Leyden to the Plymouth rock, recommended them to use "all means to avoid and shake off the name of Brownist, being a mere nickname, and brand, to make religion odious, and the professors of it, to the Christian world." † Our fathers held indeed, that every congregation is completely independent of all others as to jurisdiction and authoritative control; but not as to other forms of connection arising from common interests and reciprocal affections. They carefully cherished an intercourse of mutual respect, and confidence, and love, an interchange of counsels, and aids, and fraternal offices; which they styled "the communion of churches." The judicious and moderate opinions of our fathers are well expressed by Thomas Shepard:—"We utterly dislike such Independency as that which is maintained

* Way of Congregational Churches Cleared, p. 9, 10.

Young's Chronicles, p. 397.

by contempt, or careless neglect, of sister churches. We utterly dislike such dependency of churches upon others, as is built upon usurpations and spoils of particular churches."*

The Puritans loved church unity;—not a mere nominal and formal union, where there is neither life nor similarity; a union well compared by Leighton to that of sticks and stones when frozen together; a union consisting in a bare outward uniformity, under which is concealed the bitterest scorn and hate. They prized "the unity of the faith," and sought to keep "the unity of the Spirit in the bond of peace:" and this was nearly all they deemed important.

Great efforts have been made to effect a uniformity of government and worship, which should bring all christendom into one ecclesiastical establishment, with unvarying modes and forms. There are men whose notion of the church is like a system of gas-pipes in a great city, branching in all directions, yet meeting at last in one main trunk, which is regarded with senseless awe, and mystic veneration as "the great centre of visible unity." Very different is the Gospel view, which shows every par-

* Treatise of Liturgies, &c., p. 114. 1653.

ticular church to be built directly on Christ as the foundation, and to be no otherwise connected with other churches, except as through him who is as the common foundation of them all. So too each believer, by himself, is a branch of the true vine, deriving life and nourishment, not mediately through ramified boughs of dependence and long limbs of distant succession; but immediately from Christ himself, in whom all the branches grow, who is the only vital bond of union between them. All real Christian union circulates through him from church to church, and from heart to heart. This hallowed bond is not an indefinitely extended chain of which only the head-link fastens directly upon the mediatorial throne. Every believer is himself in Christ. The disciples are one in him, and only in him. To all of them his Spirit is imparted directly from himself; and this unites them by pervading them all.

A Catholic Christian union already exists, so far as the different denominations rest upon the true foundation. An old divine has said, "I have seen a field here, and another there, stand thick with corn. An hedge or two has parted them. At the proper season, the reapers entered. Soon the earth was disburthened, and the grain was conveyed to the destined place;

where, blended together in the barn, or in the stack, it could not be known that a hedge once separated this corn from that. Thus it is with the church. Here it grows, as it were, in different fields, severed, it may be, by various hedges. By and by, when the harvest is come, all God's wheat shall be gathered into the garner, without one single mark to distinguish that once they differed in the outward circumstantials of modes and forms."

The "high-church" temper does not accord with the genius of Congregationalism. We are not of those who are never sure that they are actually in the temple, until they find themselves perched upon its topmost pinnacle. Such as these, Dean Kennet speaks of, as having lost their Christianity in the name of the church. Luther describes them as "attributing more power to the church which is begotten and born, than to the Word which hath begotten, conceived, and borne the church." Of such men, John Cotton used to say, "They are all church, and no Christ."

SECTION II.

NATURE AND POWERS OF THE MINISTERIAL OFFICE.

The fathers of New England held that the officers of the church are of two sorts. One of these is variously spoken of as pastors, teachers, elders, presbyters, bishops, overseers, and other names indicative of the nature of their calling, and its duties. These all stand upon an equality as regards rank and authority. There is no difference among them, except such as make any man to differ from his political equals, arising from diversity of talents, attainments, or moral worth. Hence the office holds out no temptation to those ambitious aspirants, whose whole desire is to reach some station superior to that of their fellows. There is no contending which shall be greatest in the kingdom of heaven, so long as there is no such condition acknowledged there. Each looks his brother in the eye, without receiving from him the glance of arrogance, or casting upon him that of uneasy inferiority. The primitive parochial bishops of the old "standing order" in Massachusetts, look with pity on those dissenting presbyters, who sink the dignity of their office, by giving place to spiritual superiors whom the Chief Shepherd never set over them.

The Scripture view of the ministerial office is thus briefly summed up by the venerable John Cotton: "The bishops Paul speaketh of in Timothy, of whose qualification he giveth direction, (1 Tim. 2: 2—7,) he calleth them all, when he cometh to give order for their maintenance, by the name of elders. And in his epistle to Titus, the elders which Paul left Titus to ordain in every city, he calleth them bishops. Tit. 1: 5—7. Now of these he appointeth many in one city or church; not many cities or churches under one bishop, Acts 14: 23; elders in every city, Acts 20: 17, 28; many elders or bishops in the church of Ephesus, Phil. 1: 1; many bishops as well as many deacons in one church of Philippi, and that a poor one too; for Philippi was a church in Macedonia, Acts 16: 12; and all the churches in Macedonia had trial of deep poverty, 2 Cor. 8: 12." *

The deacons form the only other class of church-officers to be seen in the light of the New Testament. Their appropriate duty is, to attend to the secular affairs of the church; but being usually more eminent for active piety,

* Way of the Churches of New England, &c., p. 48.

they are chiefly looked to for advice, and expected to prepare the business which may come before the church. It is singular that, in most religious denominations, this office is either discontinued, or its nature and duties are entirely changed. In the hierarchal churches, the deacons are transferred from the charge of temporalities to that of spiritualities. They have ceased to "serve tables," and profess to "give themselves to the Word of God and to prayer." In a word, they claim to be clergymen. Moreover, they are never inducted into their office with any expectation of retaining it for life. It is not sought or conferred for its own sake; but merely as one condition of being admitted to a higher order in the priesthood. It is difficult to conceive of a greater departure from its original design, than this divinely appointed office has undergone. In the Congregational churches it is retained, and fulfills its original purposes.

We hear much in our times about the necessity of an "apostolical succession" in the gospel ministry. And truly such a succession is needful, not in form, but in fact; not in show, but in spirit. Wherever you see a "son of consolation," one "who is a good man, and full of the Holy Ghost and of faith," there you see a true successor of the apostles, so far as they can have successors on earth. It is no matter through what external source he may have derived his license or authority to preach the gospel and administer its offices; if the spirit that was in the apostles be in him, he is their fellow-laborer, and their successor in the work they wrought. Though he may have undergone no prelatical manipulations, he is qualified to serve at the altar, "by the imposition of a holier hand."

When we see a man called to the ministry by the church of God, his mind instinct with the grand truths of revelation, "mighty in the Scriptures," fervent in spirit, instant in prayer, burning with love to Jesus, and to the souls for which Jesus bled, laboriously and faithfully dispensing the bread of life to hearts hungering for the heavenly food, where is he who will coldly ask to see his commission to preach the gospel, to ascertain if it be endorsed by human sanctions? When such a ministry is blessed to the illumination of the ignorant, to the reformation of the profligate, the conversion of the infidel, the comfort of the afflicted, the edification of believers, and the salvation of hundreds and of thousands, who would care to inspect his ecclesiastical pedigree? While such a man "continues steadfastly in the apostles' doctrine and fellowship, and in breaking of bread, and in prayers," who will question the apostles' fellowship with him, and their approval of his work?

Look at Bunyan, faring so coarsely in Bedford jail, and yet with quenchless zeal exercising his despised ministry with the broad seal of heaven's approbation,—the effusion of the Holy Ghost making it effectual for the conversion of sinners and the consolation of saints. Then look at the lordly diocesan, under whose unhallowed authority that man of God was incarcerated only for doing his Master's work,—look at the "enthronized" prelate, arrayed in canonical silks and rubrical lawns, intent on worldly dignities and possessions, a stranger to the great teachings of the gospel, and hostile to its spirit. Compare the two men, the tinker and his oppressor. Then, with the Acts of the Apostles and their Epistles in your hands, ask which of the two men looks the most like their successor. Were the fishermen of Galilee, or the tent-maker of Tarsus to revisit this world, the scene of their toils and sufferings for Christ and his Church, in which of these men would they discern the clearest proofs of spiritual affinity with themselves? With which would they most readily hold communion in their ministerial offices?

When you receive the sacrament with a heart

melted in penitence, glowing with love, burning with holy desire; when you enter with your whole soul into the communion of saints; when you feed on Jesus by faith, and find that his flesh is meat indeed, and his blood drink indeed; when, in that sacred hour, heaven descends into your bosom, and all is joy and peace: say,—can you doubt the validity of the ordinance, and scruple at the official character of the administrator? No: you would say;—"God is here, and it is good for me to be here: for truly my fellowship is with the Father and his Son Jesus Christ." That man's religion is vain, who proudly rejects a ministry which God condescends to accept, and seal with his presence and his blessing. Wherever we find the most of the apostolical doctrine and the apostolical spirit, there we are sure to find the most genuine succession.

As for this ecclesiastical figment of a direct lineal succession from the apostles, we may array against it not only the opinion of our fathers, but the testimony of prelates inferior to none in learning, and as much interested as any of their brethren in sustaining the fiction, if it were possible.

The famous Dr. Hoadley, Bishop of Bangor, declared, "As far as we can judge of things,

God's providence never yet in fact kept up a regular, uninterrupted succession of rightful Bishops."* Speaking of that pretended succession, he says;—"Of which the most learned must have the least assurance; and the unlearned can have no notion, but through ignorance and credulity."† Dr. Whately, the present Archbishop of Dublin, has declared;—"There is not a minister in all christendom who is able to trace up, with any approach to certainty, his own spiritual pedigree."‡ The present Bishop of Hereford, in a charge to his clergy, says, in reference to the certainty of an apostolical succession;—"To spread abroad this notion, would be to make ourselves the derision of the world."§

The "simple faithful," and such as "occupy the room of the unlearned," are in a sorry case, if they can never take the comfort of Christian sacraments in due security, till they can decide where erudite prelates disagree. It happens, somewhat oddly, that, at least two metropolitans of the Anglican Church, Tillotson and Secker;

* Preservative against Nonjurors, p. 47, 4th ed.

† Answer to Representation by Committee of Convocation. p. 89—91.

‡ Whately's Kingdom of Christ, Essay II., Sect. 30.

§ Cited in Hall's Puritans, p. 388.

and four of its heads, James the First, William the Third, and George the First and the Second, had none but Presbyterian baptism, which is said by some to be a nullity. "So we have Bishops appointed by unbaptized heads of the church, and consecrated by prelates excommunicated at Rome," the corrupt mother of a cast-off daughter, who yet claims to inherit all her boasted exclusive privileges from that unhappy parentage. It is surely impolitic to rest the doctrines of the church, as Macaulay has well said, "on a historical theory, which, to ninety-nine Protestants out of a hundred, would seem much more questionable than any of those doctrines."* It is far better to derive our belief from the apostolical Scriptures, which are the pure fountain-head; than from any of the branches of that "muddy Tiber," the Roman succession.

The Israelites were thought to be in sad plight, when, for lack of smiths, they were forced to go down to the Philistines, "to sharpen every man his share, and his coulter, and his axe, and his mattock." It was acutely said by some of our old Puritans;—"Sure, if Christians might not have any ministers, unless ordained by the

* See an able article on "Church and State," in the Edinburgh Review for April, 1839.

popish bishops, the case were as pitiful as if sheep might have no shepherds, but such as are appointed to them by the wolves."*

Of late years the old superstitious notions of ordination seem to be regaining ground. There are many who look upon this solemnity as a sort of charm, having a magical effect to make a man, be he what he may, a true minister of Christ; and investing him with a mysterious character, and conferring on his ministrations a spiritual efficacy which cannot be secured in any other way. The first reformers and the martyrs of the reformation had juster sentiments. In the book entitled "The Necessary Doctrine and Erudition of a Christian Man," which was penned by Archbishop Cranmer as a text-book for the instruction of the common people, that blessed martyr affirms the original identity of bishops and presbyters; and contends that nothing more than mere election, or appointment, is essential to the sacerdotal office, without consecration, or any other solemnity. From a manuscript in the handwriting of the same worthy, penned with a view to further reformation in the time of Edward VI., and transcribed by bishop Stillingfleet in his Irenicum, occurs the follow-

* Modest and Brotherly Answer to Charles Herle, by Ri. Mather and Wm. Thompson, 1644.

ing explicit statement;—"*Question* 12. Whether in the New Testament be required *any consecration* of a bishop and priest, or only appointing to the office be sufficient?" "*Answer.* In the New Testament to be a bishop or priest needeth no consecration, by the Scripture: for *election* or *appointing* thereto is sufficient." Seeing that the consecrating rites of ordination are used, not of necessity, but only for decency or solemnity, it is of very little importance, comparatively, how or by whom they are performed. If the ceremonies were omitted, the ordination would be less decorous, but not less valid.

Such evangelically liberal opinions were once more common than now, in those who arrogate the episcopal function to themselves. In the reign of James the First, the bishops of Raphoe and Elphin, in Ireland, united as presbyters with the Scottish presbyterians in ordination services.* Archbishop Bancroft, though a stern persecutor of all non-conformity, and the rest of the bishops with him, owned ordination by presbyters to be valid: and, on this account, refused to reordain the Scottish presbyters who were then to be made bishops of the new dioceses in North Britain; declaring that to doubt it, was to

* Bogue and Bennett's History, vol. II. p. 411.

doubt whether "there were any lawful vocation in most of the reformed churches."* Dr. Burnet, bishop of Salisbury, thus expressed himself on this subject;—"As for the notion of the distinct offices of bishop and presbyter, I confess it is not so clear to me: and therefore, since I look upon the sacramental actions as the highest of sacred performances, I cannot but acknowledge those who are empowered for *them*, must be of the highest office in the church." †

Erasmus does not hesitate to say, that, in the time of the apostles, "Bishop, Priest, and Presbyter was all the same." ‡ But it were out of place here to relate such testimonies, which are numerously rehearsed in the books which expressly treat of these topics. Let these citations suffice to show, that our fathers were not singular in their opinions, which their strenuous adversaries had not always the hardihood to controvert. Even what has been called "lay ordination," in cases of emergency is not without the sanction of divines of the highest consideration, both in ancient and modern times. Thus Luther says;—"If any pious laymen were banished to a desert, and having no regu-

* Archb Spotteswood's Hist. p. 514.

† Vindication of the Church of Scotland, p. 310.

‡ Opera, Tom. V. Col. 652. Ed. Lugd. 1704.

larly constituted priest among them, were to agree to choose for that office one of their number, married or unmarried, this man would be as truly a priest as if he had been consecrated by all the bishops in the world. Augustine, Ambrose, and Cyprian were chosen in this manner."* Even Hooker, the boasted champion of prelatic power, was "judicious" enough in the third book of his Ecclesiastical Polity, to acknowledge boldly, that such ordinations have been often justifiable. "There may be," he says, "sometimes very just and sufficient reason to allow ordination made without a bishop. Where the Church must needs have some ordained, and neither hath nor can have possibly a bishop to ordain, in case of such necessity the ordinary institution of God hath given *oftentimes*, and may give place."

Our fathers held that the power of calling suitable persons to office, belongs to the church; and there too inheres the power of displacing such incumbents as prove to be incapable or unworthy. It is a maxim of law, that the right of divesting for good cause, goes with the right of investing.† The privilege of calling to office

* Appeal to the German emperor and nobles, given in D'Aubigne's Hist. of Reformation. II. 84.

† Cujus est instituere, ejusdem est destituere.

the first churches exercised in the very presence of the apostles. And it was many ages before this privilege was entirely wrested out of their hands by the hierarchal usurpers, who strove to exalt the clergy at the expense of the people, and acted on the principle that the church was made for the minister, and not the minister for the church. Though all the ministers were to perish in a night, the Church would still survive in the baptized fraternity ; and this brotherhood would be authorized to establish the ministry anew. It is from the Church that the ministry must come. They must be church members before they can become church ministers; and the very name of *minister*, or servant, implies the previous existence, and the appointing power, of the body to be served.

The opinion of our fathers is thus expressed by Cotton Mather ;—"Ordination they looked upon but as a ceremony, whereby a called minister was declared by imposition of hands, to be *solemnly set apart* for his ministry; and in the same rite, the assistances, and protections, and manifold blessings of the Holy Ghost in the exercises of his ministry, were solemnly implored for him. Briefly, they reckoned not ordination to be *essential* unto the vocation of a minister, any more than coronation to the being of a king; but that it is only a consequent and convenient *adjunct* of his vocation, and a solemn acknowledgment of it, with an useful and proper benediction of him in it."*

Properly the church elects her own officers; and ordination is but solemnly and formally setting apart to his duties the person so chosen. It is no charm, and exerts no magic power. It is merely opening to suitable persons that door of office which should stand closed to the unsuitable. As the church has the sole right of calling to office, this greater right involves the lesser right of directing how the ordination should be conducted, due regard being had to the requirements of the Bible. But though officers derive their calling from the voice of the church; yet the powers and privileges of office, after they are called and inducted, they derive from the appointment of Christ, who has determined in his law what they shall be. Thus it is in our civil commonwealth, which is modeled very much upon the Scriptural plan of church polity. The executive officers of the State obtain their offices by the choice of the people; but being once chosen, their duties and prerogatives are not prescribed by the popular will, but

* Magnalia Book V. Ch. XVII. Sect. 5.

by the written constitution of government. So the church appoints her ministers; but Christ appoints their duties and privileges in the Bible, the sacred statute-book of his kingdom. "The law and the testimony," describes the nature of these offices; the Church only supplies incumbents to occupy them. They who hold them are to follow only the regulations which their Lord has enacted. The Church may exclude from her ministry, and her membership such as prove themselves unworthy; for to this end the keys of the kingdom are committed to her with the tremendous power of binding on earth what shall also be confirmed in heaven. But if she attempt to exercise this "power of the keys" contrary to the decrees of inspiration, nothing is effected; for in so doing she changes the key, and an erroneous key bindeth not.* The Church can do nothing but what Christ has authorized to be done. The power committed to the Church is not legislative, but administrative. Her power is ministerial, or stewardly; and it is for this purpose, that "the keys" are hung at her girdle. Christ put a stop to law-making, when he made an end of the canon of inspiration. The matter is

* Clavis errans non ligat

forcibly expressed by Mr. Cotton, of whom a very powerful opponent remarked;—"I had a particular unwillingness to enter the lists of strife with that reverend, famous, most able, and *tight* writer." Mr. Cotton was speaking of that clause in the apostolic commission;—"Teaching them to observe all things whatsoever I have commanded you." His words are: "If the *apostles* teach people to observe more than Christ has commanded, *they go beyond their commission;* and a larger commission than that given to the apostles, neither Elders, nor Synods, nor Churches can challenge."

This matter is discussed by him with great clearness and "evidence of Scripture light" in his book, entitled "The Keys of the Kingdom of Heaven." This is, at the present day, the most important of his published writings. He here claims somewhat more of authority for the elders of the Church, than has usually been conceded among Congregationalists; and particularly he ascribes to the elders the veto power, so that they may have a negative upon the acts of the brotherhood; but no right, in any thing which concerns the latter to impose aught upon them without their consent. With this one exception as to the veto, the sentiments of this book accord with what has been generally professed by our churches, and it is marked by careful discrimination and logical precision.

Their great business of proclaiming the gospel, clothes the ministers with an influence so commanding, while rightly directed, that they need wish for no higher authority. To "labor in the word and doctrine," is to rule preeminently well, and gives the teaching elder who does it a special title to "be counted worthy of double honor." "Preaching is a principal part of governing, and Christ himself ruleth his Church by his Word."

It is something admirable that our forefathers should stamp such an independent character upon each particular church and its ministry. In so doing they rose above all the prejudices of education, and surmounted the whole force of public opinion in their times. Though born in an age of hierarchies, and bred under one themselves, they made no attempt to imitate the system here. What was there to hinder them from constituting a new hierarchy here with the potent John Cotton at its head? What was there to prevent them from endowing their churches with vast territorial possessions entailed upon them forever? They did nothing of the kind; though they had purchased to themselves a right to do so if they chose, by banishing themselves to the wilderness for the express purpose of doing as they chose. But no man would have resisted more strenuously than Mr. Cotton himself, the attempt to confer upon him the least official supremacy above his brethren. We find him refusing to be supported in any other way, than by voluntary contribution, the free-will offerings of his people.*

Following the Scripture rules and precedents, our fathers declared for the equality of all churches, the equality of all church members, and the equality of all church ministers. That "liberty wherewith Christ hath made us free," could have no stronger safeguards.

SECTION III.

NATURE AND FORMS OF PUBLIC WORSHIP.

The principal part of this duty is prayer, with its proper adjuncts of praise and confession. Our fathers held, that "true prayer is the work of God's Spirit in our hearts, teaching and ena-

* Winthrop's Hist. I. p. 121.

bling us to pour out our souls unto God in all necessities and occasions." On this account, they held that prayer should be *free;* not restricted to set forms and prescribed liturgies, to be used compulsorily at all times of devotion. They found neither Christ nor his apostles requiring any invariable forms of prayer. From this John Cotton argued, that there is "no expediency thereof to the edification of the church; unless it might be presumed, that there is some help, or means, of God's worship expedient to the edification of the Church, which never came into the heart of Christ and of his apostles to commend unto the Church." * To exact the constant use of a "stinted liturgy" when Christ exacted it not, our fathers regarded as a direct usurpation of Christ's kingly office, by imposing conditions of membership and ministry in his Church which he never decreed.

Such a liturgy, they said, was the *lethargy* of worship. It is not to be wondered at, that they sometimes spoke harshly of it, when stung to desperation by tyrannous and cruel attempts to force them, under the severest penalties, to read or hear it. "Oppression maketh a wise man mad."

---

* A Modest and Clear Answer, &c., ch. 1.

The Puritan divines could find no trace of such liturgies for the first three centuries of the Christian era. They found that the compilation of them owed its origin to the wretched ignorance of many of the clergy, who, being incapable of properly discharging this duty, had forms of prayer drawn up for their use. Such forms, the Puritans regarded as crutches for the lame ; and were willing that the lame should use them. But they knew no reason why these instruments, however handsomely turned or richly adorned, should be forced upon such as were not lame enough to need them. Thus in a speech made in 1641, in the house of peers, by Lord Viscount Say and Seal, that noble Puritan says ;—" This injunction of such forms upon all men turns that which, in the beginning, necessity brought in for the help of insufficiency, to be now the continuance and maintenance of insufficiency, and a bar to the exercise of able and sufficient gifts and graces ; as if, because some men had need to make use of crutches, all men should be prohibited the use of their legs, and enjoined to take up such crutches as have been prepared for those who had no legs ! "

The service-book having been mostly translated from the Latin missal used by the Romish priests, was the occasion of much stumbling at it by the Puritans. Even King James once described it as "an ill-said mass in English." The reason given by the compilers of the common-prayer for retaining so much of the Romish book, was a wish to conciliate the Papists, as much as possible, to the Protestant worship. And even Bishop Stillingfleet could once argue, that what was merely "laid as a bait" for the Papists, could never have been intended "as an hook for those of our own profession." But a hook they found it! and so keenly barbed, that it was not without much laceration that they disengaged it from their bleeding mouths.

They could never be reconciled to that which became the instrument of so much civil and religious despotism. They could never succumb to the pretensions of any set of men to dictate to all other men, even in distant regions and future centuries, with what petitions they should approach the throne of grace, and in what terms they shall address their Heavenly Father. To prescribe a form, they said, was stopping the course of God's Spirit, and muzzling the mouth of prayer. What can be more contrary to the free and fetterless spirit of New Testament worship, than thus to confine it to sluggish canals, with formal locks for reaching a measured elevation; instead of permitting it to flow in its natural channels as marked out by the finger of Providence, and filled by the Spirit of God? As well might we attempt to give an artificial outline to the flames upon the altar, and seek to fix them in one unvarying shape.

The inconveniences of being tied up to such a ritual were curiously illustrated during the struggle between James II. and the Prince of Orange. Though the body of the clergy favored the side of William and Mary, they were obliged to follow the liturgy, which the Archbishop, engrossed as he was by political duties, had not time to alter. The poor ministers had to keep on praying for their most dread and sovereign liege-lord, King James, that "God would confound the devices of his enemies." This was hard, both on them and the public: on them, as being forced to pray against their own wishes; and on the public, because the nation would have been ruined, if their prayers had been accepted.* During the American Revolution, it came to pass, that nearly every Episcopal meeting-house in the colonies was closed. Their ministers, inclined as they were to principles of monarchy, both in Church and State, could not vary from the prescribed forms of prayer: and the people, filled

* Life and Times of Dr Edmund Calamy. I. 201.

with the spirit of liberty, could not endure the petitions for king George, which those unalterable forms required.

No one form of prayer can be ample enough to express all the wants of the Church. It was well said by one good man ;—" If I had a prayer-book which contained all my wants, it would be so large, that I should be obliged to carry it about on a wheel-barrow ! "

In other parts of worship, such as singing the praises of God, and the preaching of his Word, our fathers had little that was peculiar to themselves. The sacraments of baptism and the Lord's Supper, they regarded as signs or emblems of the highest spiritual truths. In administering the sacraments, they used a plainness and simplicity, agreeable to the Scriptural patterns, and such as showed that they were but signs. A pompous and imposing ceremonial tends to confine the mind of the worshiper to the sacrament, as if it might have some virtue or saving efficacy in itself. But the more simple celebration constrains the worshiper to feel that these sacred things, after all, are only signs ; and thus the soul is led to look through them, and beyond them to that which is signified. Such observance is the most spiritual, and is best adapted to secure the great ends of the sacraments of grace and life.

Thus have we briefly surveyed the outlines of that godly discipline, which our fathers modeled after the pattern in the mount. The lapse of two centuries has suggested no material improvement, no closer approach to the primitive and apostolical plan. This building of God goes bravely on. Founded on the Rock of Ages, it lifts apace its rising walls, and heightens all its towers, standing in massive and enduring strength.

And when the millennial sun shall rise in cloudless glory, the fair fabric shall front the rejoicing East. Its gold, and silver, and precious stones shall reflect in mild radiance the intenser blaze of the ascending orb. Each stately pillar and graceful arch shall glow with the living light of heaven. From its open gates of lucid pearl shall burst the choral songs, which tell that God,—God in the fullness of his bliss,—is there.

CHAPTER VII.

The merits of Congregationalism. Paul's defence of himself against the charge of heresy. Application of it to the Puritans. Restoration of Christ's kingship in the Church., John Cook quoted. Recapitulation. Subject divided. I. Antiquity of the Congregational way. Study of antiquity. Excessive deference paid to the old Ecclesiastical writers. Uncertainty of Patristical traditions, illustrated by more recent instances. Remnants of the earliest fathers characterized. Retort of Irish convert. King Jamie's maxim. Luther's estimate of the "fathers." Lord Bacon's estimate. King James again. The sacred writers the best church antiquarians. John Wilkes' retort. Luther's retort. John Cotton's opinion. His opinion sanctioned by candid Romanists. What if we had lived in the third century? Connecticut ministers. II. Catholicism. What it is. S. Mather. Dr. Owen. J. Cotton. Protestation of Puritans. Two divines. Open communion, the Congregational practice. I. Mather. Cambridge Platform. J. Cotton. Gov. Winslow. John Higginson. Jonathan Mitchell. Massachusetts pastors to John Dury. Variety in unity preferable to mere uniformity. III. Spirituality. Congregationalism congenial to the "free spirit" of the gospel. Spirit and forms. Milton. Barrowe. Conder. Practical tendencies of Congregationalism. Promotes liberality. Cherishes public spirit. Favorable to liberty. Excites free inquiry. John Robinson. John Norton. J. Winslow. J. Cotton. Relation of Church and State. "The wisest of the best." Failures and successes of the Puritans.

The apostle Paul was once pleading in his own defence before Felix. It was a critical hour, and his life hung upon the event. The Jewish priests, by their hired advocate, Tertullus, had charged the Apostle as being a mover of sedition against the imperial authority, and as being a ringleader, or literally a front-rank man, of the sect of the Nazarenes. On these grounds, they demanded that he should be adjudged to death.

The Apostle, in his reply, first disposed of the unfounded charge of sedition. He then proceeded to discuss the accusation, that he was a prominent leader among the Nazarenes, which was one of the earliest names by which the followers of Jesus were known. "But this I confess unto thee, that after the way which they call heresy, so worship I the God of my fathers." While he thus frankly owns himself to be a Nazarene, he makes the acknowledgment in such a way as to take off all culpability from the fact. For he alledges, that, as a Nazarene, he worships none other than the God of his fathers; and this was a privilege which had been secured to the Jews by several of the edicts and charters of the Roman emperors. He was thus entitled to the protection of the law. He not only affirms that he was a worshiper of the God of Abraham, but that he believed the whole canon of the Jewish Scriptures; and, like the mass of that people, had a firm hope of a general resurrection.

The invidious name of *sect* or *heresy*, which the high-church party among the Jews applied to the Nazarenes, means strictly *a taking up*,—a taking up with any new-fangled opinions. This charge the Apostle could very sincerely deny. For the Holy Ghost had taught him that Christianity was nothing else but Judaism brought to its full perfection. Judaism was the acorn, whose ceremonial shell concealed the future oak. It was the germ which contained all the rudiments, as yet undeveloped, of the broad, umbrageous tree. The advent of Christ was the germination which burst the henceforth useless shell; and started the rapid growth of that tree of life, beneath whose wide and sheltering shadow the gathered nations of the earth should sit.

In the process of centuries, this monarch of the forest had nearly lost its natural growth. It was overgrown with strangling vines, and with parasites which wasted its vigor, and with noxious grafts of a nature contrary to its own. The reformers of the sixteenth century, set themselves to work as God's husbandmen, to clear away this cumbrous mass of foreign vegetation. The Church of God in England, one chief limb, was purged to a great extent: but it remained for our Puritan fathers, in the following century, to complete the work, and to present at least one living branch of the ancient tree restored to its pristine state, and flourishing in its own natural and beauteous growth.

But to drop this parable, our fathers when they went on to perfect their ecclesiastical reform, were assailed by all the forces of the hierarchy. High priests and lower priests loudly accused them before Cæsar's tribunals of heresy and sectarism. To this invidious charge the accused could reply with the Apostle :—" But this I confess unto thee, that after the way which they call heresy, so worship I the God of my fathers."

After the first English reformers had restored the *prophetical* and *priestly* offices of Christ, our forefathers conceived that the KINGLY OFFICE of Christ still remained to be restored. They sought to reform the government, as well as the doctrine, of the Church. They maintained that ordinances of man's invention are no more to be mixed up with what Christ has instituted as King, than man's dogmas are to be blended with his teachings as the great Prophet of Israel, or than man's works and merits are to be mingled with his atonement as the High Priest of our profession.

Their views were well expressed in a tract printed in 1647, by John Cook, of Gray's Inn, Barrister: from which a few quotations will be offered. " The question, truly stated, is but this,

Whether the inventions of men ought any more to be mixed with the institutions of Christ in his Kingly office, than their good works in his Priestly office." An Independent "is content to be every man's servant, so as Christ may but reign over his conscience, which if He should not, we know not where he is to reign." "He depends not on any but Christ Jesus the Head, in point of canon and command, for spiritual matters. Concerning the discipline of Christ's Church, he does no more depend upon man than concerning the doctrine; and counts it the most glorious sight in the world, to see Jesus Christ walk as King, ruling by the sceptre of his Word in the midst of his golden candlesticks." "He will not be beaten but by Scripture weapons: and in reading Scriptures, neither stretches things wider, nor draws them narrower than God has made them." We give one extract more. "He judges Christ's Kingdom to be only there where *His* laws are in force; for that county is no part of a prince's dominion which is not regulated by his laws."*

True to these principles, the "Reformists" sought, with scrupulous care, to restore the prim-

* A reprint of this sententious tract may be found in the third volume of Hambury's Historical Memorials relating to the Independents, &c.

itive and apostolical order of church administration.

In the preceding chapter we gave a brief sketch of the main features of that church government which our fathers deduced and adopted from the Bible. We showed, that they held each local church or covenanted congregation, to have entire spiritual jurisdiction within itself, to be fully competent to its own government by the rules of God's Word, and to be no ways dependent on other churches, except for reciprocal acts of kindness and assistance, as one hand may help another. We showed that they considered ministers of the gospel to be all equal in respect to official rank; to be elected and called by the Church to that great work; and to labor therein according to the instructions of the Bible, and not according to the dictates of men. Owning Christ as supreme Lord and Master, and all his disciples as free and equal subjects of his power, they looked upon the visible Church as an absolute monarchy democratically administered. We also exhibited their views of public worship,—that it should be simple in its character, and chiefly marked by unfettered freedom and high spirituality.

And now we present for consideration the

merits of this ancient, catholic and scriptural system of ecclesiastical discipline.

SECTION I.

THE ANTIQUITY OF THE CONGREGATIONAL WAY.

Far be it from us to slight the authority of antiquity, provided it be of the highest kind; namely, the oldest of which the case admits. Our pilgrim-sires contended, that their order was no *newer* than the New Testament: and that it was old enough to be coeval with Christ and his apostles, from whom it originated.

The mind takes a pleasure in coming into contact with things remote. It delights to travel back into the distant ages of the past, tracing up usages to their origin, and standing at the far off fountains from whence the streams of custom have come rolling down to our times. These pilgrimages of the mind amid the vestiges and monuments of perished centuries are full of pleasure and profit.

> "Nor rough and barren are the winding ways
> Of hoar antiquity, but strewn with flowers."

But there is no study which requires more

plain and practical good sense. Imaginative minds become, as it were, spell-bound by the venerable aspect of the past; and under its wizard-wand, lose the power of discriminating between veritable truth and monastic fabling, between actual occurrences and legendary lore. It requires great soundness of judgment to traverse the dim vista of ages almost unstoried, where the solemn shapes loom up with awful port, "and frowning in the uncertain dawn of time," subdue the soul with a superstitious reverence. To reduce these shadowy forms to their real dimensions requires a keen-eyed caution and strong-minded solidity, which have not been the endowments of every enthusiastic scholar. One of the most laborious and sensible of England's older antiquarians has said;—"Abating only Holy Writ, it is as impossible to find antiquity without fable, as an old face without wrinkles."

As to the fathers of the church, as they are called, or the ancient ecclesiastical writers, it is not easy to see any good ground for the deference which has been paid to their authority in theological questions. Especially when we consider how easy it is on any such question to quote fathers against fathers, and councils against councils, it is strange to observe the respect which has been paid to the contradictory responses of these ambiguous oracles. Neither the Church nor any of its members in those earlier times had any promises of supernatural aid and guidance, more than the Church and its members may have now. Nor had they any more right to decree for our observance, articles which Christ never sanctioned, than we have to do such a thing for them that shall live a thousand years hence.

It is said, that the Greek and Latin fathers are valuable witnesses as to the belief and practice of their own times, and so they are. But it is not from their times, nor from any times except those of the apostles, that we are to take our pattern.

It has been said too, that, as these antiquated authors lived nearer to the apostolic age than we, they must have preserved a nearer and more correct tradition of what the apostles did. But let us take a case with which we are familiar. It is not two hundred years since the first settlers of New England were living. They have been succeeded by five or six generations of their descendants, an educated people, deeply interested in the events of that period, and abounding in printed books relating to it. Now suppose we were to go about among our people, collecting all the traditionary information which remains among them, relative to the affairs and practices of the first settlers of this soil. Can any one believe, that out of the materials so amassed, the web of an accurate and veritable history could be woven? It is certain that a narrative drawn up from such sources of information must abound in gross mistakes and absurd fabrications.

What reliance, then, can be placed upon traditions received by men who lived and wrote two hundred years after the apostles:—traditions preserved among a people of whom the mass was exceedingly ignorant and unintelligent; and of whom the superior part was by no means marvelously enlightened. The credibility of such traditions, to which the art of printing had not rendered its important aid, must ever be extremely suspicious. Take a case nearer our own day, drawn

> "From that Brabantine field,
> The proudest field of fame."

The battle of Waterloo was the most eventful passage of arms which has been decided for many a long century. For historical purposes it is important to know at what hour of the day, that fearful strife of embattled nations began. And yet of all the numerous actors in the scene who have attempted to narrate the order of its events, scarce two agree as touching that one simple matter of fact. How vague and unsatisfactory, then, must be any uninspired tradition, especially if it have been long unwritten? The reflecting mind cannot content itself with such dubious authority in matters of the highest moment. And why should it seek contentment there, when the apostles themselves, "moved by the Holy Ghost," committed to infallible records all the traditions which *they* wished to hand down to the successive ages of the church?*

The writings of the fathers were extravagantly over-estimated in their own times, and ever since. Read the remains which have come down to us from the apostolic age. The largest of these are the epistle of Barnabas, the fellow laborer of St. Paul; and the "Shepherd" of Hermas, the same, perhaps, to whom St. Paul addressed a salutation in the last chapter of his epistle to the Romans; and the epistle of Clement, also saluted in the same chapter. Whoever expects to find in these pieces much of the Pauline stamp of thought and diction, will be sadly disappointed. The epistle of Barnabas is a tedious and tasteless affair, full of poor and senseless conceits, and absurd allegories. As for the "Shep-

*2 Thess. 2: 15, and 3: 6.

herd" of Hermas, if any one were to read it, without knowing but what it might be some modern production, he would throw it aside as the scribbling of some miserable driveler. The epistle of Clement the Roman, addressed to the Corinthian Church, is a moderately respectable performance; but, in respect to richness of gospel truth and evangelic fervor, immeasurably inferior to the epistles of St. Paul to the same Christian community. In reading these writings of men whom the apostles had known and taught, we cannot but feel the conviction deepened, that it was the inspiration of God which enabled the apostles to teach in a strain of doctrine and argument at least a whole heaven above these their disciples and followers.

If we learn from these earliest fathers so little, indeed nothing, in addition to what instruction the New Testament gives, we may well give up the expectation of being made much wiser by the study of the vast and voluminous remains of the later fathers. When the Romish priest objected to the Irish convert to protestantism, that he was not acquainted with the opinions of the fathers, it was wisely retorted by the latter, that he had done what was much better; he had prayerfully studied the *grandfathers*,—Matthew, Mark, Luke, and John. He who has informed himself of the low state of education and literature during the centuries which preceded the Protestant reformation, will hardly persuade himself that the authors of those times are fit to be the teachers of the nineteenth century. Their traditions will have no weight whatever. Even that royal sophomore, James I., had sense enough to say;—"In all usages and precedents, let the times be considered wherein they first began; which [times] if they be weak or ignorant, it derogateth from the authority of the usage, and leaveth it for suspect." According to this principle, the fathers will be but dubious guides. A more thorough and systematic view of the doctrines and duties of Christianity can be derived from the volumes of Dr. Dwight, than from all the ponderous tomes of Chrysostom, and the huge lumbering folios of Augustine beside.

It is true that the works of the later fathers, who lived when the primitive simplicity was lost from sight amid the accumulating inventions of superstitious or aspiring men, are generally favorable to hierarchy and its proud pretensions. But the few genuine documents which have descended to us from the first three centuries, fully substantiate the Congregationalism of the Puritans. And this explains the treatment which the ancient writers have received from the divines of the Anglican Church. That treatment led Chillingworth to say, that "those divines account the fathers to be *fathers* when they are *for* them, and *children* when they are *against* them." Martin Luther, who was learned in this sort of lore, was so perplexed by the many discrepancies and puerile fancies which abound in those old ecclesiastical writers, that he cast them aside in despair. He once said;—"When God's Word is by the fathers expounded, construed and glossed, then, in my judgment, it is even like to one that straineth milk through a coal-sack, which must needs spoil and make the milk black." In five different places of Lord Bacon's works, he repeats the sentiment;—"Time seemeth to be of the nature of a river or flood, that bringeth down to us that which is light or blown up, and sinketh and drowneth that which is solid and grave." Were it not for his lordship's charity, he might have felt some suspicions, that antiquity, after all, has sent down to us the best it had.

The Puritans were too stiff-kneed to succumb to the decisions of uninspired men, whether ancient or modern. But they were ready to bring their church polity to the test of antiquity, provided it should be the oldest antiquity of all. In reply to such as imagined that their churches dropped out of the clouds some time in the sixteenth century, they could adopt the language of King James at the Hampton Court Conference;—"I know not how to answer the objections of papists, when they charge us with novelties, but by telling them, that we retain the primitive use of things, and only forsake their novel corruptions."

And truly, if antiquity is to decide the point, let us go back of the old writers to the older Bible. The Acts of the Apostles is a far purer and more ancient record than the most antiquated of the church histories; and the apostolical epistles are far safer and more venerable documents than the mustiest relics of what schoolmen and churchmen have penned. Why should we examine the subject of the Church's constitution by the feeble tapers of human wisdom, when we may bring it at once to the sun-light of revelation. If you were suffering from a painful disease, and the physician were to offer you a vast variety of remedies, of which some would help you a little, and others would help you more; and if he were to hold out one which would afford instant and permanent relief, would you not promptly reject the others, and insist upon receiving that which will give immediate health and soundness? And why should we be dallying with the fathers, when the blessed Bible so far exceeds them in every thing in which they can be supposed to benefit us? Well has it been said by a living divine;—"The Bible is older than the fathers,—truer than traditions,—wiser than councils,—more learned than universities,—more orthodox than creeds,—more infallible than popes,—more authoritative than priests,—more powerful than ceremonies,—more reliable for the world's salvation than any thing or every thing else under the heavens."

When the Papist asks the Congregationalist;—"Where was your church before the Puritans set it up?" we might answer as John Wilkes, the celebrated sheriff of Middlesex, did in a similar case. He retorted on the Papist;—"Sir, did you wash your face this morning?" The Papist answered, somewhat sullenly, in the affirmative. "Well then," rejoined the witty sheriff, "where was your face before it was washed?" This question was shrewdly put: for let the popish corruptions be thoroughly washed off, and the popish pollutions be purged away, and the fair face of the Church will reappear in its primeval beauty. Or we may answer briefly with Luther to the priest who scornfully asked;—"Where was your Church during so many long centuries?" To whom the bold reformer promptly replied;—"My Church was where yours never was,—in the Bible!" Holding fast this inviolable charter of the city of God, we may appeal from men who reject us, to God who owns us. We may appeal in the language of the prophet;—"Doubtless thou art our Father, though Abraham be ignorant of us, and Israel acknowledge us not: thou, O Lord, art our Father, our Redeemer; thy name is from everlasting."

Nothing can be more sound than John Cotton's remark;—"That must be true which was primitive; and that must be primitive which is from the beginning. There is no false way," he adds, "but what is an aberration from the first institution." He followed this principle till it led him to say;—"The way of Independency hath been bred in the womb of the New Testament of the immortal seed of the Word of truth, and received in the times of the purest primitive antiquity."* He looked upon no other mode of ecclesiastical discipline to be "so ancient as the way of our Congregational government of each church within itself, by the space of three hun-

* Way of Congregational Churches, p. 9, 1648.

dred years. Congregational discipline was instituted by Christ and his apostles."* This opinion is sanctioned by some of the best informed historians in the communion of the Church of Rome. Of this, any one may find sufficient proof in the authorities cited by Moshein. To these may be added the testimony of the monastic writers of church history, known as the Magdeburg Centuriators. "But, whoever will look through the approved authors of this age, will see that the form of government was quite democratical. For individual churches had equal power, as to purely teaching the Word of God, administering the sacraments, excommunicating heretics and offenders, choosing, calling, ordaining, and for just reasons deposing again, their ministers, and assembling conventions and synods."† Du Pin, a doctor of the Sorbonne, and a man of rare learning and candor, speaking of the first three centuries, acknowledges in general that the mode of church government was altogether of a popular cast; and then adds;—"After all, it must be confessed, that the discipline of the church has been so extremely different, and so often altered, that it is almost impossible to say any thing pos-

* Way of Congregational Churches, pp. 93,94. Also Prop. I., in survey of Church Discipline.

† II Cent. Chapter 7. Title, De Consociatione Ecclesiarum.

itively concerning it."* The hierarchal way of ruling is most evidently not aboriginal in the church, but is the fruit of antiquated changes.

Why, then, should we cling to practices which, however antiquated, were in their origin innovations upon the pristine usage. "An error by continuance of time can never become a truth, but only the more inveterate error." Suppose that, with our present views and feelings, all Christendom were to urge some novelty upon us for our adoption—should we feel under the slightest obligations to adopt it? Certainly we should not. But suppose that, with the same correct views and feelings which we now have on the subject, we had lived in the third or fourth centuries; when so many hierarchal novelties were introduced and imposed:—should we have felt obligated to submit to them then? We certainly should not. Why then should we submit to the same things now? They were innovations when they were first introduced, and they have been mere innovations ever since. Our stal-wort sires trampled them in the dust, and strode ruthlessly over them all, that they might plant their feet upon the rock of truth, *that rock of primitive formation.* They were solicitous

---

* Biblioth. Patrum. Tom. III., Cent. III., p 183.

to base the fabric of their churches on none but a scriptural antiquity: for they knew that the Word of God is not only ancient of days, but that it "abideth forever." They embraced the maxim of Peter Martyr, admitting "nothing *without*, nothing *against*, nothing *beside*, nothing *beyond*, the divine Scripture."

A recent writer, who has treated these subjects with consummate ability, tells us truly, that "this has ever been the great principle of Puritanism: that God's Word is the sole and sufficient standard of faith and duty." Nearly a century after the landing of the Pilgrims, an assembly of Connecticut ministers, in setting forth their general assent to the Savoy Confession of Faith, as containing the system of doctrine which they embraced,—deemed it important to preface that act and confession with these words, worthy to be written in broad letters of living light. "We do not assume to ourselves that any thing is to be taken upon trust from us, but commend to our people the following counsels: 1. That you be immovably and unchangeably agreed in *the only sufficient and invariable rule of religion*, which is THE HOLY SCRIPTURE, the fixed canon, incapable of addition or diminution. YOU OUGHT TO ACCOUNT NOTHING ANCIENT THAT WILL NOT STAND BY THIS RULE; AND NOTHING NEW THAT

WILL. 2. That you be determined by this rule in the whole of religion. That your faith be right and divine, the Word of God must be the *foundation* of it, and the authority of the Word the *reason* of it."* Such noble advices will never be heard from the lips of the assertors of priestly power. Their only study is to circumscribe the rights of the people, and restrain them from that use of "private judgment," which God requires of every accountable being.

SECTION II.

THE NEW ENGLAND CHURCH GOVERNMENT AS RESPECTS CATHOLICITY.

BY catholicity is meant that generous and loving spirit, by which every Christian embraces, in the arms of his charity, every other Christian as a brother in the Lord. The true apostolical catholicism rejoices in the unity of the spirit, rather than in the unity of outward forms. It fondly cherishes a union of hearts, even where there may be little uniformity of practices. It is like the law of vegetative life, which is the same

* The Puritans and their Principles, by Rev. E. Hall, 8vo., 1846, p. 150.

in all plants, and marks them as the subjects of one and the same kingdom; and yet developes itself in an endless variety of production. It has been eloquently said;—"The productions which adorn the paradise of God, from the loftiest cedar of Lebanon, to the lowliest plant which flourishes beneath its shade, are all pervaded by the same great principle of spiritual life; are all sustained by the same influences of heaven and of earth; all imbibe living moisture from the same dew and shower; and rejoice in the genial radiance of the same celestial sunshine: but they, at the same time, present endless varieties of form and structure, of fruit and flower, of leaf and fragrance."

Now the catholic spirit of the gospel manifests itself by recognizing the same spirit wherever found, and however diversified the aspect it wears. With false and anti-christian churches, it has nothing to do. Its repugnance to them is as strong as its attraction toward every evangelical communion. Hatred of heresy is a twin flower with love of truth. They bloom on a common stalk. But while the brotherly love of the gospel shrinks, like the sensitive plant, from the hateful contact of soul-destroying errors, it unfolds all its leaves to the congenial breath of purity. "We reckon it our distinguishing honor," writes

Samuel Mather, "that, of all the reformed churches, we are the most *distant* from the church of Rome, and the most *conformed* to the churches in the days of the apostles and of primitive christianity."

As respects this genuine catholicity, the Congregational churches may affectionately invite comparison with their sister-churches of other names. And this comparison is invited, not as challenging an invidious superiority in this or any other point of excellence; but as kindly craving their own proper dues.

Dr. Owen and our fathers took an open and honest stand. "Unless," say they, "men can prove that we have not the spirit of God, that we do not savingly believe in Jesus Christ; that we do not sincerely love all the saints, his whole body and every member of it; they cannot disprove our interest in the Catholic Church." * Our fathers regarded their communion as one purified branch of the true church catholic. This was the extent of their modest claim. They did not pretend to unchurch other communions. They did not pretend, that they had an exclusive monopoly of covenant blessings. They asserted nothing more than a right to regard

* John Owen, D. D., "Of Schism," &c. chap. IV., sec. 19.

themselves as one province of the kingdom of Christ, in which their Lord's laws were more strictly enforced than elsewhere. Listen to the declaration of John Cotton;—"We cannot but conceive the churches in England were rightly gathered, and planted according to the rule of the gospel: and all the corruptions found in them since, have sprung from popish apostacy in succeeding ages, and from want of thorough and perfect purging out of that leaven, in the late times of Reformation in the days of our fathers. So that all the work now, is not to make them churches which were none before, but to reduce and restore them to their primitive institution."* The treatise from which this is quoted, though prepared by Mr. Cotton, appears to contain the results of his brethren's deliberations. From this, and innumerable other testimonies of the same character, it is evident, that our fathers were equally ready to assert their own rights, and to admit the just rights of others, to a place in the house of God.

In the time of James I., in a pamphlet called "A Protestation of the King's Supremacy, made in the Name of the afflicted Ministers, &c.," the demands of the Puritans were thus expressed.

* "Way of the Churches in New England, &c., p. 111."

"All that we crave of his majesty and the State, is, that with his and their permission, it may be lawful for us to worship God according to His revealed will; that we may not be forced to the observance of any human rites and ceremonies. So long as it shall please the king and parliament to maintain the hierarchy or prelacy in this kingdom, we are content that they enjoy their state and dignity: and we will live as brethren among the ministers that acknowledge spiritual homage to the spiritual lordships, paying them all temporal duties of tithes, and joining with them in the service and worship of God so far as we may, without our own particular communicating in those human traditions which we judge unlawful."* Two distinguished divines, during a process against them for non-conformity, sent a letter to the Archbishop and the other ecclesiastical members of the High Commission, in which occurs the following language;—"Conscience is a tender thing, and all men cannot look upon the same thing as indifferent; if, therefore, these habits seem so to you, *you are not to be condemned by us;* on the other hand, if they do not appear so to us, *we ought not to be vexed by you.*" †

* Cited in Neale's History, Part I., chap. 1.

† Ib. Part II., chap. 4.

In matters of this nature, the Congregational churches not only profess catholic principles, but practice them. And a square-foot of performance is worth an acre of profession. Thus our churches lovingly receive the members of other evangelical churches to occasional, and even stated communion at the Lord's table, and in other religious ordinances. We receive such members into our own churches without rebaptism: and their ministers without reordination. We cordially unite with them in associated effort to extend the Redeemer's kingdom on the earth. Our men and our means have contributed to the gathering of thousands of churches which are attached to other denominations. What more could we do to evince a catholic spirit of fraternal union with all who "hold the Head, from which all the body, by joints and bands having nourishment ministered, and knit together, increaseth with the increase of God?"

Our churches, in respect to Catholicity, will compare to great advantage with other religious communities. These, in general, will not suffer any to enter, or to continue among them, especially ministers, unless they will conform to every practice, however unessential, or however inconsistent with scripture rule. But we, on the contrary, are ready to receive from them, without rebaptism or reordination, all whom Christ has received. We exact no conditions of them but what Christ has required. We demand their assent only to such points as all evangelical Christians admit to be vital to the faith, and fundamental to salvation. In minor points, every one is left to the liberty of his conscience, and to the freedom of his own judgment: "admitting," as Dr. Increase Mather has said, "of all those, though in different persuasions about lesser points, of whom it may be judged, in reasonable charity, that Christ has received them to the glory of God." To which he adds this impressive remark;—"Our foundation is in these holy mountains!" *

This is that chief grace of charity which bids us to "*love* alike, though we do not *understand* alike." It teaches us to exercise the mild judgment of Christian love in the reception of such as are weak in the faith. The Cambridge Platform directs, that "such charity and tenderness is to be used, as the weakest Christian, if sincere, may not be excluded nor discouraged. Severity of examination is to be avoided." † Dr. Samuel Mather says;—"My great grandfather, the holy and learned Mr. Cotton, once

* "Elijah's Mantle," p. 16.

† Chap. XII., sec. 3.

said to his congregation, that, if any person, though a poor Indian, should step forth and say, 'I love the Lord Jesus Christ in sincerity and truth,' and should testify his willingness to walk according to the gospel, though his defects were great for ignorance and the like, he should be for admitting him to the Lord's table."

The liberal character of Congregationalism is opposed to a strenuous pressing of uniformity. The rules of outward uniformity must bend, when necessary, to the maxims of spiritual unity: even as the precepts of the ceremonial law gave way, when they occasionally conflicted with the requirements of the moral law. "We require no man," says Mr. Cotton, "to swear to our church government: nor ever did, that I know. Neither do we so much as require, that they should profess their approbation of our government." * These sentiments of one whom Dr. Goodwin calls "that apostle of his age," are sanctioned by his fellow-laborers and fellow-sufferers. Thus in Winslow's "Brief Narration," numerous examples are given of free communion as practiced by the Leyden, Plymouth and Massachusetts churches, in their intercourse with other reformed churches. "For we ever placed,"

* Holinesse of Church Members, p. 29.

he says, "a large difference between those that grounded their practice on the Word of God, though differing from us in the exposition or understanding of it, and those that hated such Reformers and Reformation, and went on in anti-christian opposition to it and persecution of it."* Those good men felt that they, so far as it rested with them, were in full communion with all that was right anywhere in the Christian world. As they phrased it, they were "for every reformed church, so far as it is reformed." They steadily repudiated the charge, so industriously alledged against them, of being separatists. Said the excellent John Higginson of Salem, when preaching the annual election sermon in 1663;—"The end of our coming hither was a *reformation* only of what was amiss or defective in the churches we came from: from which we made no separation, but a *local* secession only into this wilderness, with true desires and endeavors after a more full reformation according to God's Word."† In the same discourse, he affirms;—"This was, and is, our cause, that Christ alone might be acknowledged by us, as the only Head, Lord, and Lawgiver in his Church; that his written Word might be

* Young's Chronicles, p. 391.

† The Cause of God and his People, p. 11.

acknowledged as the only rule; that only and all his institutions might be observed and enjoyed by us; and that with purity and liberty, with peace and power." * In carrying out this design, our fathers distinguished between things necessary, and such as were in their nature indifferent. So Higginson, on the same occasion, taught;—"In matters divine, where we have a clear command, with Moses, we must not yield an hoof: but in matters human, standing upon extreme right may prove to be extreme wrong." †

Jonathan Mitchell, a kindred spirit, preached the annual election sermon for 1667. He then took occasion to remark;—"The good old nonconformists were very zealous for reformation, and yet always steadfast enemies to separation: those two may well consist, and they left us a good example therein." ‡ So too John Norton, and all the other Massachusetts pastors, in their letter to Mr. Dury, have said;—"We chose rather to depart into the remote and unknown coasts of the earth, for the sake of a purer worship, than to lie down under the hierarchy, in the abundance of all things, but with the preju-

* The Cause of God and his People, p. 13.

† Ib. p. 21.

‡ Nehemiah on the Wall in troublous times, p 28.

dice of conscience. But that in flying from our country, we should renounce communion with such churches as profess the gospel, is a thing which we confidently and solemnly deny." * If this formal disclaimer, to which they subscribed their names, will not absolve them from the charge of having made a breach in the catholic unity, then no compurgation could avail.

In a letter written by Oliver Cromwell to the Long Parliament, he says ;—" All that believe, have the *real* unity, which is the most glorious; because inward and spiritual, in the Body, and to the Head. As for being united in outward forms, commonly called Uniformity, every Christian will for peace-sake study and do, as far as conscience will permit. And for brethren, in things of the mind we look for no compulsion, but that of light and reason." † The Protector's modern vindicator has said ;—" To Cromwell, perhaps as much as another, order was lovely, and disorder hateful; but he discerned better than some others what order and disorder really were. The forest-trees are not in 'order' because they are all clipt into the same shape of Dutch dragons, and forced to die or grow in that way; but because in each of them there is

* Letter to Mr. John Dury, p. 11.

† Carlisle's Letters and Speeches of O. Cromwell; Letter XV.

the same genuine unity of life, from the inmost pith to the uttermost leaf, and they do grow according to that!"

We rejoice in that unsurpassed catholicity of our churches, which allows a happy liberty to them and to their members. And if only there be a spiritual and internal union, why should the entire visible church be hewn down to the dead level of a dull uniformity? Variety in unity is the law of heaven. In God himself is seen the adorable mystery of trinity in unity, investing his "lightning-shrouded seat" with threefold glory and indivisible perfection. The living creatures about the throne, variously represent distinct powers and virtues. The burning seraph, and rushing cherub are glorious in their several make and mould. From the brightest archangel to the fairest of the ministrant spirits, there are many gradations of might and beauty, even as one star differeth from another. And among the ransomed saints from earth, there are patriarchs, who, before the flood, were ripening in wisdom and grace for a thousand years: and with these is the infant which "fell on sleep" with the baptismal dew still fresh upon its brow. In that day, when God shall "make up his jewels," and shall set them in his crown, it will be gemmed with a gorgeous variety of precious stones, not cut to one size or shape, nor tinged with the same unvarying hue. The sapphire shall blaze along with the diamond, and the ruby blush between.

SECTION III.

THE MERITS OF CONGREGATIONALISM AS RESPECTS SCRIPTURAL SPIRITUALITY.

This mode of church government affords full scope to the genius of our religion. The free spirit of Christianity is impatient of human fetters and trammels. It delights in breaking yokes, and disinthralling minds which have been subjugated by sin and by worldly usages. It constitutionally dislikes the confinement of imposed forms when they are not of divine appointment.

The grace of God in the heart is a leaven, which works from within outwards. It is an inner life, which, instead of adapting itself to the outward shape it inhabits, conforms *that* to itself. As the solid bones of the head fit themselves to the conformation of the soft brain, so the outward forms of our religion should take their shape from the animating and assimilating spirit within. And to pursue the figure,—when the brain is dead, so is the skull; which yet long retains its shape after the other has turned to dust and disappeared. Even so are all the forms of religion empty, dead and defiled, when its life and spirit are departed. They are like the death's head and cross-bones in the monkish cells, fitter to inspire disgust than to awaken piety. They belong to the charnel-heaps of a lifeless and decayed religion.

The gospel holds up spiritual worship in opposition to that which is merely formal; and therefore it favors a simple worship, not encumbered with pompous observances which would be likely to catch the mind of the worshiper, and detain it in a ceremonial net-work. The ancient attempts to adorn the plain apostolic worship with a magnificent ritual, resulted, as Milton says, "in drawing down all divine intercourse between God and the human soul into an exterior and bodily form; till nearly all the inward parts of worship, which issue from the native strength of the soul, ran lavishly to the upper skin, and there hardened into a crust of formality." It is certain, that the Congregational discipline and worship must languish, so far as the power of godliness declines. To maintain our father's system in its vigor and efficiency, there must be a high degree of spirituality in the

Church, a pervading, vital and active piety. This fact is one chief recommendation of that system, and is an evidence of its primitive and scriptural character.

There is a strong propensity in man to merge the life and spirit of religion in its outward forms. When we see persons who were once apparently converted to God under the simple ministrations of the gospel, betaking themselves at last to a punctilious observance of rites and ceremonies, we cannot but lament their degenerate piety. How applicable to them the language of the apostle to those of his converts who were relapsing into Jewish formalities;—"Are ye so foolish? having begun in the Spirit, are ye now made perfect by the flesh?" May we ever have grace to escape such vassalage; for vassalage it is, though its serfs are so prone to be proud of their shackles.

One of the oldest Puritans, a martyr to the cause of spiritual Christianity, has said;—"Let us, for the appeasing and assurance of our consciences, give heed to the Word of God, and by that golden reed measure our temple, our altar, and our worshipers; even by these rules whereby the apostles, those excellent, perfect workmen, founded and built the first churches."*

* Barrow's Brief Discovery, &c., 1590, p. 7.

The Bible Christian cannot but feel a deep interest in an ecclesiastical order which studiously seeks to arrange itself "according to the pattern in the mount." "The Word of God," says a modern writer of note, "is our only rule, in the sense both of a law and a standard; a rule sufficient, as opposed to all deficiency; exclusive, as relates to any other than the Divine authority from which it emanates; universal, as embracing all the principles of human actions; and ultimate, as admitting of no appeal from its decisions."*

He who is born of the Spirit, is born free: and where the Spirit of the Lord is, there is liberty. Jesus is the grand Liberator of souls, bringing deliverance to the captives, and the opening of the prison doors to them that are bound. The children of Zion come of no servile parentage: for "Jerusalem which is above is free, which is the mother of us all." In short, the religion of Jesus is the emancipation of the soul. And so, by a sort of natural necessity, it calls for forms of government as liberal and popular as disinthralled humanity can wish. The spiritual and scriptural forms which our fathers adopted, fully meet this requisition.

---

* Protestant Nonconformity, by J. Conder, 1818, II., p. 318.

In considering the merits of this ancient, catholic, and spiritual system, we must not omit to speak of its practical tendencies.

We are led to notice the tendency of Congregationalism to enlarge and liberalize the heart. Paying little regard to the sectarian peculiarities of other communions, it is the less apt to overestimate any peculiarities of its own. Hence it is the more ready to enter into such leagues and alliances as may foster the communion of churches, without destroying their just independence.

As it was best adapted to those *primitive* times of the gospel wherein it began, so will it be found best adapted to those *ultimate* times of promise, in which the gospel shall prevail over all the earth. "Such is the truly liberal and catholic spirit, which characterizes the principles of Congregationalism, that if the millennium were to commence tomorrow, there would be no need of modifying or changing any one of those principles. It sets up no exclusive terms of communion; it insists upon no outward forms, or unessential rights as conditions of Christian fellowship. It receives *all*, whom there is evidence to believe Christ has received. On this ground, our churches without relinquishing or altering any one principle of their organization, or polity, might admit to their communion the whole world, converted to Christ, and extend the hand of fellowship to *all* Christians of whatever name or denomination. But on the principle of the Episcopalians, the millennium can never come till the whole world become Episcopalians ; and on the principle of the Baptists, the millennium can never come till the whole world become Baptists; and on the principle of the Papists, the millennium can never come till the whole world become Papists : but on the principle of the Congregationalists, the millennium may come at any time, and they be prepared to enter into the spirit of it, and embrace in the arms of Christian fellowship, all who love the Lord Jesus Christ in sincerity and truth, however much they might differ in certain points of form and ceremony."*

Congregationalism cherishes public spirit, or that disposition which prompts men to exertions and sacrifices for the general good. Whatever happy pre-eminence New England may enjoy, is owing to the public spirit diffused throughout her population. And it has been diffused mainly by the influence of that ecclesiastical order which makes every member of the church feel that he has something to do for others, as well as for

* Tribute to the memory of the Pilgrims, by Joel Hawes, D. D., p. 87, 88.

himself. This is from the remoter source whence are derived those acts of ample munificence for which New England is famed. The generous benefactions of individuals and of congregations to promote education, beneficence and piety at home and abroad, are chiefly emanations from the deep-seated springs which our church polity has opened. This is the rod of God which smites the rock, and causes streams to gush forth in the desert, and make it glad.

It is obvious that such a church polity elevates the popular rights, and favors civil liberty, and imparts the capacity to maintain it. People who have been bred to self-government in an independent church are competent to govern themselves in a free commonwealth. A people so trained must feel an equal aversion to despotism and to anarchy. They can have no sympathy with either. They will be the sworn foes of oppression, and the fast friends of order. The sense of individual responsibility which has been aroused in the church-meeting, will not sleep in the town-meeting. It will ever be a wakeful sentinel by the watch-fires of freedom. It was on their system of independent churches, that our forefathers based the political liberties of the country. And the foundation which they laid has stood firm as the granite hills. And so long as that system of independent churches shall predominate in the land, so long will it be morally impossible for aspiring hierarchs to tread religious freedom in the dust.

Freedom of inquiry after truth is eminently promoted by Congregationalism. It tells every man that he is personally responsible to God for knowing the truth. It tells him, that he cannot throw off his responsibility on pope or patriarch, on proud prelate or plain pastor, on the living or the dead. The mind once stirred up to investigation, will never more lie down submissive to the dictates of authority. "Human reason, when the fit of free inquiry is upon it, is in truth like a wild beast; the smaller the cage in which you confine it, the more fiercely it will rage." The wiser course is, to place the truth fully in the way, and then give full scope to the speaker. If he be seeking sincerely, he will soon close with the obvious truths which will meet him on every side. If he be not sincere in his seeking, he will at least, escape the deeper debasement of an enforced and groveling hypocrisy. God himself, all-powerful as he is, wins the heart by persuasion rather than by force.

In exemplifying the liberal character of our

principles, we cannot help quoting the well-known farewell address of John Robinson to the Plymouth colonists. "He was very confident that the Lord had more truth and light yet to break forth out of his holy Word. He took occasion also miserably to bewail the state and condition of the Reformed Churches, who were come to a period in religion, and would go no further than the instruments of their Reformation. As, for example, the Lutherans, they could not be drawn to go beyond what Luther saw; for whatever part of God's will he had further imparted and revealed to Calvin, they will rather die than embrace it. And so also, saith he, you see the Calvinists, they stick where he left them; a misery much to be lamented; for though they were precious shining lights in their times, yet God had not revealed his whole will to them; and were they now living, saith he, they would be as ready and willing to embrace further light, as that they had received. Here also he put us in mind of our church covenant, at least that part of it whereby we promise and covenant with God and one another, to receive whatsoever light or truth shall be made known to us from his written Word; but withal exhorted us to take heed what we received for truth, and well to examine, and compare it and weigh it with other Scriptures of truth before we received it. For, saith he, it is not possible the christian world should come so lately out of such thick anti-christian darkness, and that full perfection of knowledge should break forth at once." * These noble instructions given by the Leyden pastor, have been grossly perverted to sanction a reception of errors which that great man had examined and rejected long before. Even in his day, so far from being regarded as "new light," they were renounced as "old darkness."

We have another example of the liberal character of Puritanism, which is not less noble than Robinson's address, and is not so liable to be wrested into a plea for the adoption of error. It occurs in the dedication of John Norton's "Orthodox Evangelist;"—"Even fundamental truths, which have been the same in all generations, have been, and shall be, transmitted more clear from age to age in the times of reformation; until that which is perfect is come, and that which is imperfect be done away. The truth held forth is the same; though with more of Christ, and less of man. Such addition is no

* Gov. Winslow's Report in Young's Chronicles, p. 396.

innovation, but an illustration: not new light, but new sight." And such has been the case. Theologians, without tampering with what our forefathers held to be fundamental articles of faith, have greatly improved the mode of presenting and illustrating the articles of their belief. They have not changed the mirror: but by raising its polish, it reflects a clearer image of the truth.

As Governor Winslow once remarked, "the primitive churches are the only pattern which the churches of Christ in New England have in their eye, not following Luther, Calvin, Knox, Ainsworth, Robinson, Ames, or any other, further than they follow Christ and his apostles." Mr. Cotton, no less than the good Robinson, lamented the disposition of the reformed churches in Europe to keep at a stay just where their reformers left them, rather shrinking back than going further in the path of improvement. These are some of his words;—"Who knoweth not, they have all been more studious and tenacious of what form the doctrine, and worship, and discipline was left unto them, than inquisitive after further light; yea, sometimes more inclinable to look back unto Egypt, than to hasten toward Canaan?—Seeing our faith resteth only on the Word of the Lord, and his Spirit breathing therein; and the Word hath promised that more and more light shall break forth in these times, till Antichrist be utterly confounded and abolished; we shall sin against the grace and worth of Truth, if we confine our truth to the divines of present or former ages."* This breathes the free spirit of Christianity, which can be confined to no narrower limits than the infinite fullness of eternal truth.

Our forefathers favored the same principles of government both in church and state. It is said that democracy necessarily runs into aristocracy, because the executive power must fall into the hands of a few. But our forefathers desired that this aristocracy should not rest upon the accident of birth, nor the circumstance of wealth, but upon the personal merit of individuals. They desired so to order the Church and State, that, by the natural course of events, wisdom and goodness should rise to their proper elevation, and have their proportional ascendency in the direction of affairs. What Governor Winthrop desired, was to have the administration consigned into the

* A Modest and Clear Answer, &c., 1642, chapter X.

hands of the *best* of the people, and of the *wisest* of these. This scheme reminds us of the promise which Ion exacted from his senate ;—

> "Promise, if I leave
> No issue, that the sovereign power shall live
> In the affections of the general heart,
> AND IN THE WISDOM OF THE BEST."

It may be said, that this sounds very well in theory or in poetry; but cannot be completely attained in practice. To this we answer, that our fathers were "not of those who dream of perfection in this world." But they set their standard of perfection high, and sought to approximate to it as nearly as they could.

And how did they expect to make the sovereign power reside "in the wisdom of the best," when every thing was left depending upon the popular elections? They sought to effect this result, by making the people see that their own interest required it should be so. To bring the people at large to understand this truth, that their interests required that the powers of government should be lodged in the hands of "the wisest of the best," our fathers depended upon the school master and the minister. In other words, they would have the people trained up to an intelligent piety, which would, almost with certainty, so use the elective franchise, that the best qualified men should be chosen to office. Hence their zeal for education, and the early provision they made for the college, and common and grammar schools. That the whole body of the people should be educated was essential to the success of their political theory. For the same reason did they take such anxious care to provide for an able and orthodox ministry. They would allow no town to be settled, except by a number competent to form a church, and to sustain a minister of the gospel. Hence too the laws which required all the people to attend on public worship. All this was done with a view to accomplish the object of their social compact, by training up a people who shall have good sense and good feeling enough to commit the political power to the wisest and best men among themselves. The success of our fathers' plans has, in a good measure, justified their theory of government, and most of their methods of securing its beneficial operation.

In reviewing the result of their labors, our feelings are divided between exultation over the happy fruits of their pains, and sorrow of heart that so much of the good seed they planted has failed to ripen. Great has been the measure, both of success, and of disappointment. And as each, in rapid alternation, has engaged our thoughts,

> A wild and variant blast our bugles sent,
> Wandering 'twixt notes of triumph and lament.

But after making every allowance for numerous partial failures of their schemes, the grand social and moral experiment of our Puritan fathers has been blessed with eminent prosperity. It is true, that many tares are growing in the field, but great will be the wheaten harvest that shall be reaped. The world cannot turn up to the face of day, for the sun to shine upon, a region more flourishing and fair than ours. Surely God "hath not dealt so with any nation." To His name be all the praise!

But the chief reward of our fathers' pious toils is yet to come. They looked for more than earth can give; they expected all that heaven can grant. They are not doomed to disappointment. They shall obtain the prize they sought, on the saints' coronation-day. Oh then,—when the hosts of heaven shall be marshaled in their bright array, when the universe of God shall be assembled to the sight, when "all the pomp and prodigality of heaven" shall be lavished forth to grace the scene,—while angel trumpets and celestial harps shall ring out their melodious thunderings, while jubilant alleluias, like the surges of the voiceful sea, shall burst in all the tumult of delight,—then shall those holy men receive their triumphal garlands whose amaranthine wreaths shall never fade away. Robed in light, and throned in glory, they shall reign with the Son of God forevermore.

CHAPTER VIII.

Difficulties in the way of our forefathers. Relation between Church and State. Abstract of Mosaic laws. Codification of laws. Relation between the ministers and the magistrates. Mr. Norton. Mr. Cotton's sermon. Letter to Lord Say and Seal. First association of ministers. Mode of supporting the ministry. Public spirit of those times. Roger Williams banished. Controversy between him and Mr. Cotton. Revival of religion in First Church. Church discipline. Anne Hutchinson. The Antinomian controversy. John Wheelwright. Sir Henry Vane. Mr. Cotton implicated. Discovers the deceptions practiced upon him. Regains his good standing. General Court. Offence at Mr. Wilson's sermon. Offence at Mr. Cotton's speech. Rowland Hill. Mr. Wheelwright condemned. First synod held in New England. Eighty errors condemned. Mr. Wheelwright banished. Mrs. Hutchinson admonished. She recants. She relapses. Is excommunicated. Banished. Her unhappy end. Mr. Cotton writes against Mr. Barnard and Mr. Ball of England.

The enterprise in which our fathers were here engaged, when Mr. Cotton joined them, was one of great difficulty, as well as great importance. They had some general ideas, derived from their sacred oracle, the Bible, of the nature of the free government, in the Church and in the State, which they wished to set up. But they were sorely perplexed in trying to reduce those ideas into practical forms. It was a novel undertaking. They had no experience of other men to guide them. They were pioneers. They were to strike out a new path, through jungle and through forest, to reach the high and glorious results toward which they were looking. But, at the outset, they were themselves confused in the intricate and untraveled maze. They were at a loss to find the due bearings and proper starting points.

At this juncture Mr. Cotton came to their aid. To them he seemed like that other John, who was the Lord's herald :—"the voice of one crying in the wilderness, 'Prepare ye the way of the Lord, make his paths straight.'"

He never attained to the great conclusion, to which the present age has come, that there ought to be an *entire* separation of Church and State. But he led the way to it, by taking a position much nearer to it than that which was then occupied by the Christian world. He taught, that the ecclesiastical power is totally distinct from the civil power; and that, though they be closely connected, they are never to be confounded. This distinction prepared the way for their separation. Mr. Cotton thus expressed himself on the subject. "God's institutions, such as the government of church and commonwealth be, may be close and compact, and coordinate one to another, and yet not confounded. God hath so framed the state of church government and ordinances, that they may be compatible to any commonwealth, though never so much disordered in his frame. But yet when a commonwealth hath liberty to mould his own frame, I conceive the Scripture hath given full direction for the right ordering of the same, and yet in such sort as may best maintain the well-being of the church. Mr. Hooker doth often quote a saying out of Mr. Cartwright, though I have not read it in him, that no man fashioneth his house to his hangings, but his hangings to his house. It is better that the commonwealth be fashioned to the setting forth of God's house, which is his church, than to accommodate the church frame to the civil state."*

In following out these sentiments, the colony, where "the commonwealth had that liberty to mould its own frame," could not fail to conform to the republicanism of the Congregational church polity in which our fathers believed.

---

* Hutchinson's History of Mass., vol. 1, p. 437.

As all the freemen of this new-born republic were church members, it was thought that the law of God ought to be their rule in civil affairs. The General Court desired Mr. Cotton to draw up an abstract of the laws of Moses, omitting such as were of temporary obligation, and in their nature peculiar to the Jewish polity. This service he performed, and the fruit of his labor was many years after printed at London by William Aspinwall, in 1655. From this transaction some malicious joker has taken occasion to say, that our fathers voted that they would be governed by the laws of Moses, till they could find time to make better. The jester had *personal* reasons, no doubt, for disliking the Mosaic legislation, which is very severe upon slanderers and such as bear false witness. Mr. Davenport gives the following correct account of the matter. "Considering that these plantations had liberty to mould their civil order into that form which they should find to be best for themselves, and that here the churches and commonwealth are complanted together in holy covenant and fellowship with God in Christ Jesus, he did, at the request of the General Court in the Bay, draw an abstract of the laws of judgment delivered from God by Moses to the commonwealth of Israel, so far forth as they are of *moral*, that is, of perpetual and universal equity among all nations, especially such as these plantations are: wherein he advised that Theocracy, that is, God's government, might be established, as the best form of government, where the people that choose civil rulers are God's people in covenant with him."*

Mr. Cotton's abstract was not adopted. Another drawn upon the same general principles, but with numerous deviations, some of them important, obtained the preference. It was printed in London in 1641, and has been supposed to be the joint labor of Mr. Cotton and Sir Henry Vane.†

This was soon superseded by another body of laws of the same general character; but with a much better arrangement. It is remarkable, that the statutory system which was eventually adopted, was a code of laws systematically arranged under one hundred heads. It has been one of the chief commendations of the mighty mind of

---

* From a manuscript life of John Cotton by Mr. Davenport, quoted in Hutchinson's Original Papers, p. 161.

† Reprinted Mass. Hist. Soc. Collec., 1st Series, vol. V. p. 171, &c.

Napoleon, that he was the first in modern times to apply the principles of plain practical common sense to the subject of legislation. That great man anticipated that "his fame in the eyes of posterity would rest even more on the code which bore his name, than on all the victories he had won." It has become the basis of the legislation of half of Europe. Within a few years the same method has been adopted in several of our States, and it has resulted in that recent revision of the statutes of Massachusetts, by which a chaos of laws was reduced to order and consistency. It is wonderful to find that this last great improvement, the codification of laws, was discovered and put in practice in this colony more than two centuries ago: and our learned modern citizens have, unawares, reverted to the method of their fathers. The honor of this boast of legislation belongs to the Rev. Nathaniel Ward, the witty and pious minister of the ancient town of Ipswich; and also a student of the science of law.*

Mr. Cotton advised the people to persevere in their design of setting up a Theocracy, or divine government over a Christian commonwealth.

* Ward's Code is reprinted in the Collections of Massachusetts Historical Society, 3d series, vol. VII., p.—

His plan was, to have the public affairs administered agreeably to the principles and requirements of revealed religion, by executive officers appointed by the free election of the people. The people were to choose their own governors and other magistrates: and these officers were to govern themselves by the instructions of the Word of God. God, speaking by his Word, was to be owned as chief Lawgiver and supreme Head of their community. They who are disposed to laugh when they see the legal enactments of our ancestors backed up with texts of Scripture, may as well save half a smile for Lord Bacon, and other of the highest judicial functionaries of England, who, in those times often confirmed their decisions in the same manner. Whoever will turn over the older parliamentary debates, will find the haughtiest cavaliers in the House of Commons, triumphantly clinching an argument by appealing to Holy Writ. And doubtless, when the prophecies are more completely fulfilled in the coming of the kingdom of God on earth, the day will come round again, when it will be deemed meet for Christian people to regulate their political affairs by scriptural principles.

As one result of this attempt in our colony, the ministry was brought into a very close alliance with the magistracy. For both the ministry and the magistracy, the people cherished a religious veneration. Nor were they jealous of the intimate relations of their temporal and spiritual rulers, so long as the keys of power remained in the hands of the people by means of the elective franchise, both in Church and Commonwealth. Whenever any disposition to engross undue authority was betrayed, the people, notwithstanding their profound respect for their leaders, always promptly applied the never-failing remedy.

Good Mr. Norton says;—"It was an usual thing, henceforth, for the Magistrate to consult with the ministers in hard cases, especially in matters of the Lord; yet so, as notwithstanding occasional conjunction, religious care was had of avoiding confusion of counsels: Moses and Aaron rejoiced, and kissed one another in the mount of God."

As an illustration of this matter, we may refer to an affair which took place in September, 1634. Mr. Hooker and many of his friends, who had at first settled in Newtown, were anxious to remove to Connecticut. Much opposition was made to their removal: and the two coordinate branches of the General Court came into very serious collision. Neither branch would yield to the other. In this painful emergency the whole Court appointed a day of fasting and humiliation, which was observed in all the congregations. A few days after, the Court met again. Before proceeding to business, Mr. Cotton preached from Haggai, 2: 4;—"Yet now be strong, O Zerubbabel, saith the Lord; and be strong, O Joshua son of Josedech the high priest; and be strong, all ye people of the land, saith the Lord, and work; for I am with you, saith the Lord of hosts." In his sermon the preacher severally described the strength of the magistracy, ministry, and people. Thus the strength of Zerubbabel, or the magistrate, is his official power and authority: the strength of Joshua, or the minister, is the purity of his life and teaching; and the strength of the people is their liberty. The preacher went on to show, that, in matters of common concern, each of these three estates in the first instance, had a negative voice upon the doings of the others; and yet that the ultimate resolution ought to be in the whole body of the people. The sermon closed with an answer to all objections, and a solemn declaration of the people's right and duty to maintain their true liberties against any unjust violence or aggression. This discourse gave extraordinary satisfaction. All animosities and difficulties vanished, the various conflicting interests were reconciled, and all hands went to work vigorously, unanimously and peacefully from that day. Alluding to this affair, the reverend historian, Hubbard, says;—"Mr. Cotton had such an insinuating and melting way in his preaching, that he would usually carry his very adversary captive after the triumphant chariot of his rhetoric." It was in accordance with the views expressed in that "political sermon," that he said on another occasion;—"Purity preserved in the church, will preserve well-ordered liberty in the people; and both of them establish well-balanced authority in the magistrates. God is the author of all these three."*

It was another effect of his all-subduing persuasiveness, that certain men of distinction who, in the heat of the recent controversy, had spoken disrespectfully to some of the magistrates, "being reproved for the same in open court, did gravely and humbly acknowledge their fault."

* Letter to Lord Say and Seal.

The first association in Massachusetts was formed by the ministers of Boston and the vicinity about the year 1635. It met once in two weeks at the houses of the members. The usual business was the discussion of some important theological question. This association was, by some, regarded with a godly jealousy, lest it might, at a future day, encroach on the liberties of the people. The experience of more than two centuries has proved that this was a needless jealousy. The associations of Massachusetts, both local and general, have been highly useful and influential. At the same time, the independence of the churches has suffered no infringement.

Mr. Cotton's disposition to popularize the whole administration of religious affairs showed itself in the manner in which he chose to receive his salary. He insisted that it should be derived from the free-will offerings of the people. Once each Lord's Day, at the close of public worship, every member of the congregation who felt disposed to contribute to the support of the gospel, walked up to the elders' seat, where one of the deacons received the offerings. The proceeds were deposited in a public chest, out of which

Mr. Wilson and his colleague received for their support one hundred pounds per annum. Considering how much greater was the value of money in those days, none of our ministers are now more amply maintained. The grace of God was bestowed on the First Church of Boston, even as, of old, on the churches of Macedonia; so that, " in a great trial of affliction, the abundance of their joy and their deep poverty abound ed unto the riches of their liberality."

Nor were the pastors, on their part, less disinterested. Not to speak of the proverbial generosity of that whole-souled man, Mr. Wilson, we find, that, when subscriptions were made for charitable purposes, Mr. Cotton's donation would equal that of the wealthiest of his flock. In effecting his settlement here, he incurred expenses amounting to eighty pounds, which, at that period, was a pretty round sum. But when the people wished to reimburse it, he declined the offer, as not being necessary in his circumstances.

Indeed there is no trait more admirable in our fathers, than their wonderful public spirit, and the readiness of individuals to make personal sacrifices for the general good. When people elsewhere marvel at the public and private munificence of the citizens of Boston toward all objects of literary, philanthropic and religious interest, we can say that they came honestly by this ennobling disposition, for they derived it in its full strength from their Calvinistic progenitors.

Most of the colonists who were men of property greatly impaired their estates by the sacrifices they made for the common cause. They were ever prompt to extend to each other a helping hand. Thus, when Governor Winthrop, neglecting his own affairs in his diligent service of the public, met with severe losses, the people spontaneously presented him with five hundred pounds.

The early part of Mr. Cotton's ministry here was disturbed by some violent storms of controversy. After these tempests had "wrought themselves to rest," there followed many calm and peaceful years.

In 1635, Roger Williams was banished from the colony. The merits of this controversy will be discussed in another chapter. Let it here be said, however, and that with all respect for the memory and character of that "fiery Welchman," that the action of our fathers in this matter is capable of a good defence : and that the condemnation they have generally received has been excessive and unjust. The matter is now mentioned merely with reference to Mr. Cotton's share in the transactions.

While the magistrates had the case of Mr. Williams under consideration, Mr. Cotton, with the neighboring ministers, whom the accused had once professed to hold in the highest veneration, presented a request that the civil authorities would stay their proceedings till the elders "had in a church-way endeavored his conviction and repentance." The ministers hoped, that it was not from seditious principle that Mr. Williams had acted ; but from a misguided conscience, which they expected to be able to set right. The magistrates acceded to the proposal of the ministers ; but the governor, who too well understood the "nature of the creature," foretold to them ;—"You are deceived in the man, if you think he will condescend to learn of any of you." When other measures failed, and Mr. Williams was banished, Mr. Cotton wielded his pen in behalf of the magistrates. He published a letter concerning the power of the civil magistrate in matters of religion. The banished man replied to this letter; and also published a tract against the "Bloody Tenent of Persecution" for the cause of conscience. Mr. Cotton rejoined with another, entitled, "The Bloody Tenent washed and made White in the Blood of the Lamb, being discussed and discharged of blood guiltiness by just defence, in answer to Mr. Williams; to which is added a reply to Mr. Williams' answer to Mr. Cotton's letter." His opponent retorted with a treatise, styled, "The Bloody Tenent yet more bloody by Mr. Cotton's endeavor to wash it white in the Blood of the Lamb, &c." Here the dispute ended, as is usual in such cases, each party satisfied that he had the best of the argument.

For three or four years in the beginning of Mr. Cotton's ministry, the internal prosperity of his church was unexampled; and would, at this day, be regarded as a powerful *revival.* There were more conversions and admissions than in all the other churches of the colony. Many persons of profane and dissolute lives were surprisingly reformed, and received into the bosom of the church. The discipline, admirably administered under the pastor Wilson and the ruling elder Leveret, was of singular benefit to the congregation. There were many "gifted brethren" into whose lips the Spirit of grace was poured, to the great edification and profit of the whole body of which they were members, which was in danger of being "exalted above measure through the abundance of the revelations."

But clouds of thick darkness soon overcast the sunny prospect, and poured down their torrents, accompanied with the withering flash and the terrifying thunder. All at once the field, which was waving with such goodly harvest, was found to be sown with tares. Noxious weeds crept into that well-watered garden of gracious plants, and "roots of bitterness springing up troubled them, and thereby many were defiled."

The prominent instigator of this mischief was a daughter of Eve, named Anne Hutchinson. She was probably a pious woman; and certainly an artful one. On the ground of the apostle's direction, that the elder women should teach the younger, she used to convene large numbers of females at her house, where she instilled into them the doctrines of antinomianism in their most demoralizing form. That she was worthy of the heaviest *ecclesiastical* censures, no competent judge of such matters can doubt. The justice of the civil disabilities under which she was eventually placed, must be considered elsewhere.

Her most active supporter was Rev. John Wheelwright, her brother-in-law, who preached, as an assistant, within the extensive bounds of the Boston church, which then included Braintree, where he principally labored. His partizans urged to have him associated as colleague with the other ministers : but Mr. Cotton evaded the connection, on the ground that Mr. Wheelwright was an unsafe and violent man, and apt to raise questions of doubtful disputation.

Another of Mrs. Hutchinson's helpers was Sir Henry Vane, then a very young man, and newly arrived in the colony, where, by his grave and dignified demeanor, he wonderfully took with the people, stealing their hearts, like Absalom, from their beloved Winthrop, whom he speedily supplanted in the chair of state. By his connection with the female heresiarch, he lost his popularity, and his office, and soon returned to England. He there acted a very conspicuous part during the civil wars, resisted Cromwell's assumption of the protectorate, and was a staunch Genevan republican to the last. He died as a political martyr, being beheaded, at fifty years of age, for high treason against the ever-treacherous Stuarts. He is a striking instance of that late retribution by which posterity reverses the judgment of former times. The ablest literary arbiters of the present day, proclaim this person, once so much abused, as one of the moral heroes of his eventful times, as a colossal champion of popular rights, and both as a civilian and theologian, of vast and varied abilities. As a writer of prose in that age of great thinkers and authors, they announce him to be inferior only to the matchless Milton, and scarcely second even to him. That great poet has paid him a tribute sufficient to enrich his memory for many an age, in the following sonnet "to Sir Henry Vane, the younger."

"Vane, young in years, *but in sage council old,*
Than whom a better senator ne'er held
The helm of Rome, when gowns, not arms, repelled
The fierce Epirot and the African bold;
Whether to settle peace, or to unfold
The drift of hollow states, hard to be spelled;

Then to advise how War may, best upheld,
Move by her two main nerves, iron and gold,
In all her equipage: *besides to know*
Both spiritual power and civil, what each means,
What severs each thou hast learned, WHICH FEW HAVE DONE:
The bounds of *either* sword *to thee* we owe:
Therefore on thy firm hand Religion leans
In peace, and reckons thee her eldest son."

Upheld by these powerful supporters, Mrs. Hutchinson was enabled to raise a terrible commotion in the community. They had the address to procure, for a time, the countenance of Mr. Cotton. This they did, by giving him such explanations in private conversation, as satisfied his unsuspicious nature of the orthodoxy of their sentiments. Captivated by their ardent zeal and high professions, he gave heed to these "seducing spirits" for a time. But when, to his consternation, the vail of duplicity was thrown aside, he was shocked to find that he had unwittingly lent the sanction of his name to opinions so dangerous and corrupt. Upon this, the Antinomians charged him with dissembling, holding one set of opinions in the pulpit, and another in private discourse. This is the only transaction of Mr. Cotton's life which seems to have given serious offence to his brethren, who charged him with wavering and timidity.

His only fault, however, appears to have been the too great facility with which he suffered persons whom he had held in the highest estimation, to delude him as to their real sentiments, and to father their errors upon him. As soon as he was disabused, he exerted himself to repair the mischief. He publicly lamented his fault, in that he had slept in false security, while the enemy was sowing tares. In a letter to Mr. Davenport, he says ;—"The truth is, the body of the island is bent to backsliding into error and delusions : the Lord pity and pardon them, and me also, who have been so slow to see their windings, and subtle contrivances, and insinuations in all their transactions." Governor Winthrop gives this testimony of him, that, "finding how he had been abused, and made, as himself said, their stalking-horse, (for they pretended to hold nothing but what Mr. Cotton held, and himself did think the same,) did spend most of his time, both publicly and privately, to discover those errors, and to reduce such as were gone astray." Among others reclaimed by his efforts was Robert Lenthal, the minister of Weymouth.

Long afterwards, on a general fast-day, "Mr. Cotton, in his exercise that day at Boston, did confess and bewail, as the churches, so his own security, sloth and credulity, whereupon so many and dangerous errors had gotten up and spread in the church; and went over all the particulars, and showed how he came to be deceived; (the errors being framed in words so near the truths which he had preached,) and the falsehood of the maintainers of them, who usually would deny to him what they had delivered to others." * He was sufficiently humbled for a fault which appears to have been only the amiable infirmity of a heart too generous and confiding. When his eyes were opened to the duplicity which had been practiced, he spared no pains that he might rectify his mistake, and was very successful in arresting the spread of the evil. "By that means," says Hubbard, "did that reverend and worthy minister of the gospel recover his former splendor throughout the whole country of New England, with his wonted esteem and interest in the hearts of all his friends and acquaintance, so as his latter

* Savage's Winthrop, I. 253 and 280.

days were like the clear shining of the sun after rain."

Nearly the whole of the members of the church who resided within the present limits of Boston, favored the cause of Mrs. Hutchinson at the outset, with the exception of the pastor Mr. Wilson, Governor Winthrop and two or three others. This small minority had on its side all the ministers in the colony, except Mr. Wheelwright and Mr. Cotton; and nearly all the laymen of note. In this contest, so violent and almost unintelligible, it is surprising to see the same church, retaining as its ministers, those who were accounted the heads of the opposing parties. This fact, far more than any argument, evinces the prudence and Christian temper of the two men.

The principal errors of the Hutchinsonians were, first, the denial that sanctification is, in any sense whatever, an evidence of justification: and secondly, the assertion that the Holy Ghost dwells personally in every believer. Sir Henry Vane must needs go a little farther, and maintain that the Holy Ghost is united to the believer, in the same manner as the divine nature is united with the man Christ Jesus.

The General Court took up the matter: though Rev. Hugh Peters sharply rebuked Governor Vane, and plainly hinted that if the civil authority would limit its action to "the things that are Cæsar's," "the things that are God's" would go on much more quietly.

The Court, having the matter under consideration, called for the opinion of the ministers. In the morning Mr. Cotton preached on the disputed points to general satisfaction. In the afternoon, Mr. Wilson made a lament over the dark and distracted condition of the churches, and the divisions occasioned by the newly broached opinions. At this speech, Mr. Cotton, with Governor Vane and others took deep offence, and called upon the pastor to retract his expressions. Mr. Wilson, supported by the firm hand of Governor Winthrop, declined to give the satisfaction required. The contention threatened to wax sharp between them: but at last the wisdom and gentleness of the two ministers calmed the murmurings and mutterings which were ready to burst forth in a storm of strife. The next time Mr. Wilson preached, he was so happy as to give contentment to all.

As is usual in such cases, one error led on to

another, heresy begat more heresy, and schism necessitated further schism. The ministers questioned Mr. Cotton on a variety of articles: and though most of his replies were satisfactory, others were not thought to be sufficiently explicit and unequivocal. Expressions and phrases were weighed and dissected with astonishing scrupulosity. Though Mr. Cotton was not to be shaken from his honest belief, yet neither was he betrayed into rashness.

A ship, with passengers, was about to sail for England. "Tell our transatlantic friends," said the teacher, "that all our strife is about magnifying the grace of God. Some seek to exalt the grace of God *towards* us; and some, the grace of God *within* us." Mr. Wilson, hurt at this, replied that he knew of neither elders nor brethren among their churches who did not labor to magnify the grace of God in respect to both justification and sanctification, or the grace of God both toward us and within us. As the people understood the matter of difference, the pastor, according to the nature of his office, naturally insisted on sanctification as "the grace of God within us;" or gracious works, and experimental godliness. And the teacher, as the nature of his office might easily incline him, insisted more on justification, as the free grace of God towards us, pardoning us, not for our works or any thing in us, but solely for the sake of Christ. Each of these worthy divines was full in the faith of both these points: but to either point a relative importance was assigned by one of the ministers beyond what the other would allow. Perhaps this unprofitable dispute was never better disposed of than by the excellent Rowland Hill, who once said in a sermon;—"If I were asked which I loved the most, justification or sanctification:—I would answer like the little children, when you ask them which they love best, father or mother? They will tell you, 'I love them both best.'"

At their session in March, 1637, Mr. Wheelwright was tried before the General Court for a highly inflammatory sermon preached on a fast day. He was adjudged to be guilty of sedition and contempt of Court, though Governor Vane and a few others entered their protest. There was a reluctance to proceed to the passing of sentence. The case was deferred to the next Court, and Mr. Wheelwright was recommended to the care of the Boston church, which had interposed a petition in his behalf. Meanwhile the discussions between the ministers had narrowed the ground of controversy, till it was reduced to a mere hair-line, of such fineness as to require the nicest sort of metaphysical eye-glasses to discern any room for further difference of opinion.

When the Court was again convened, Mr. Wheelwright confronted his judges with all possible boldness. He and his partizans had been so insolent and violent, as to injure their cause: but they were encouraged by some new arrivals which brought fresh strength to the antinomian standard. Their fanatical zeal blazed out in all directions, with flaming extravagances which fired inflammable minds. Some were deranged with joys, and others with despair. The public excitement and distress was becoming intolerable. Days of fasting and prayer were observed with reference to the sad condition of affairs.

At a conference of ministers and elders held on the 30th of July, harmony was restored between Mr. Cotton and the other ministers: but Mr. Wheelwright, who was present, continued impracticable.

On the 30th of August, the first synod ever held in New England, was held at Cambridge. All the pastors, teachers and elders in the country were present. They were boarded at the public charge, by which also was defrayed the traveling expenses of the members from the colony of Connecticut. This synod condemned eighty or more different errors, which had been set afloat in the community: Mr. Wheelwright remaining as pertinacious as ever. This condemnation was signed by all the members, except Mr. Cotton, who appears to have scrupled at the condemnation of two of the points specified.

On the 2d of November the General Court assembled at Cambridge. After their long forbearance, finding all their attempts to reconcile Mr. Wheelwright unavailing, and feeling that a continuance of these dissensions absolutely endangered the existence of their little commonwealth, which was almost shaken to pieces thereby, they proceeded to banish him from their society. His sister, Mrs. Hutchinson, after a very singular trial of two days' duration, was also voted to be "unfit for their society," and required to leave it. Mr. Wheelwright went, with many of his followers, and founded the town and church of Exeter, N. H. From thence he soon after removed to Wells in Maine: and after five or six years' absence, he owned his errors, made his retraction, and was restored to a residence in Massachusetts.

The unhappy woman who had fomented such a disturbance, after a short imprisonment, was set at liberty. But returning to her old course of agitation, she was summoned before the whole congregation on a lecture day, when her errors were enumerated and condemned, and a solemn admonition was read to her by Mr. Cotton, who decidedly reproved the disposition of the woman who had once been his most ardent admirer.

She then resided a while in Mr. Cotton's family, where he and Mr. Davenport labored to convince her, and bring her to repent of her errors. They so far prevailed with her, that she made a written recantation of most of her antinomian heresies; but in language so equivocal, as failed to satisfy the church. In an oral explanation she made a general confession of her delusions, so humble and penitential, that they began to hope that she was really about to be reclaimed. But the moment they began to touch upon particular points, she became as wild as ever: and involved herself in such contradictions as amazed and alienated the last of her supporters and advocates. All hope in her favor being now abandoned, a motion was made for her excommunication. The long-suffering church, feeling a lingering tenderness for their erring sister, and something of horror at the thought of passing that dread sentence, still hesitated to take the step. At last, the resolution was adopted, and the gangrened limb was stricken from the body.

After lingering with her friends awhile, she departed to an island in Narragansett Bay, which her husband and others had purchased of the Indians. Here they were ever starting some monstrous or foolish notion:—such as, that women have no souls, that morality is antichrist, and that the devil and the Holy Ghost had an indwelling with every believer. Her husband dying about six years after, she again removed into the limits of the Dutch colony beyond New Haven. Here, in the following year, she came to the end of her earthly sorrows under the Mohawk scalping-knife. She perished with all her family of sixteen persons, except that one daughter was carried into captivity.

This protracted controversy being thus brought to a close, Mr. Cotton found leisure to write a reply to a treatise which a Mr. Barnard in England had published against the mode of gathering the churches in this country. Mr. Cotton, in this year 1638, also replied to a defence of liturgies by Mr. Ball.

Thus this faithful soldier of the cross, ever valiant for the truth, had scarce panted through the toils of one sharp conflict, before he girded himself for fresh encounters. And, doubtless, it was no small relief, to turn from the struggle within the camp to meet an adversary abroad.

CHAPTER IX.

Mr. Cotton's success in the ministry. His influence in the community. Instances. Women's vails. Independent spirit of the people. Instances. Morality of the colony. Mr. Cotton invited to return to England in 1641. Again next year to the Westminster Assembly. Congregationalists in the Assembly. Mr. Cotton declines going. Survey of the sum of Church Discipline. Other writings on the subject. Synod of 1643. Synod of 1646—8. Cambridge platform. Mr. Cotton in the family. Family altar. Sabbath keeping. T. Shepard. Letter to N. Rogers. Hospitality. Benevolence to Church of Segetea. Learning. Reading Calvin. Habits of study. Manner of preaching. Luther. Roger Clap. Fast days. Controversial writings. Correspondence, N. Rogers, O. Cromwell. Carlyle. Mr. Cotton's personal appearance. Pulpit delivery. Equanimity. Patience under abuse. Cause of his death. Last labors. Prepares to die. Closing scene. Funeral obsequies. Dwelling-house. Will. Houses of worship. Baptisms. Admissions to the church. Mr. Cotton's children. His grand-children. Ministers and preachers to the Indians. Children of Mr. Cotton who died before him. The Mothers. Mr. Cotton's widow. Woodbridge's elegy.

After his troubles in connection with Mrs. Hutchinson's disturbances, which so afflicted him that he seriously meditated a retreat from the colony, Mr. Cotton passed the rest of his days in peace and high esteem. His labors in the pulpit and elsewhere were exceedingly great; and the power of God mightily attended them, and crowned them to the conversion of numerous souls, and the edification of thousands. Under the wise counsels of the noble and devout Winthrop in the State, and those of Mr. Cotton in the Church, the community prospered to such a degree, as to make the grateful inhabitants apply to them the words of the Psalm,—"Thou leddest thy people like a flock by the hand of Moses and Aaron."

Mr. Cotton knew how to touch the keys of the human heart, so as to draw out responsive and accordant notes. He played this complicated organ with a master's hand: and though he found it sometimes sadly out of tune, his skill would often blend the jarring sounds in surprising harmony. The church which he governed, with one or two exceptions, so peacefully, was organized of very discordant materials. Many of the members were strongly inclined to most of the forms of the national church of England, in which they had been bred; and others were speculative and adventurous reformers, who scarce knew how to be subject to any settled rule. But the patient sagacity of their teacher was marvelously successful in training them to habits of agreement and order.

A few instances are recorded which may serve to show the extent of his influence. In 1634, the people of Boston chose a committee for the division and distribution of the town lands, and purposely omitted to place any of the magistrates on the committee. Mr. Cotton soon persuaded them, that it was more according to order, to refer such affairs to the civil elders of their Israel. And so they unanimously agreed to go into a new election, agreeably to his views.

In 1639, when the decays of their first rude place of worship, and the growth of the congregation, made it necessary to rear another, there arose a warm dispute as to the spot where it should stand. Their Teacher interfered with such success as to reconcile their opinions upon a point, which, above all others is apt to rend a congregation in sunder. The new edifice cost a thousand pounds, which this poor people cheerfully paid, without assessment, by voluntary contribution.

At an election held in 1641, it was proposed, that two of the deputies, who had fallen into low circumstances, should be dropped in favor of wealthier men. The Teacher, hearing of the project, generously, but prudently, condemned it at his next weekly lecture, in which he maintained, that, if old and faithful officers had grown poor in the public service, instead of being discarded, they should be relieved at the public expense. The reproof was felt, and had its proper effect.

In another case he proved that even the arbitrary fashions of female apparel could not withstand the weight of his solid counsels. Roger Williams and Mr. Skelton had persuaded the female part of their congregation at Salem, that it was a religious duty for all women to wear vails in public worship. Mr. Cotton went there to preach on the Lord's day. He was much struck at the oriental aspect of things in the congregation, so different from the customs of the English people: and in his forenoon instructions, he effectually took the vail from off the understandings of the ladies, and so enlightened their minds thereby, that they all appeared in the afternoon without any vail upon their heads. And so that fashion passed away.

But it would be the height of injustice to our free-spirited ancestors, to suppose that there was any thing servile in the profound deference they usually paid to the suggestions of their civil and ecclesiastical leaders. When occasion required, they were not slow to show a stubborn independence with which it would not do to trifle. Thus in 1634, the people felt apprehensive, that, by re-electing Winthrop, they should make way for a Governor for life. Mr. Cotton, then at the height of his popularity, in a sermon before the General Court, on whom the choice devolved, taught; "that a magistrate ought not to be turned out without just cause, no more than a magistrate might turn out a private man from his freehold, without trial." No noise was raised about this dangerous doctrine; but, at that same election, they turned out Winthrop, and put in Dudley. Next year they ousted Dudley, and put in Haynes. The year after, they left off Haynes, and put in Vane. And all by way of practically showing their dissent from the doctrine, that an elective magistrate has any thing like a freehold tenure of his office. In 1639, the Governor and magistrate ventured to nominate three persons to fill vacancies in their board; leaving the people, however, as they said, "to use their liberties according to their consciences."

And the people *did* use their liberties according to their consciences. They chose never a man of them. These were days, when "king Caucus" did not reign so despotically as now.

Such instances, rightly considered, are equally honorable to all the parties. It shows that the extreme deference ordinarily paid to their leading men, was not a blind and slavish submission; but a free and intelligent homage to their preeminent wisdom and worth.

Such was the state of morals in those days, that of twelve hundred men under arms on a training day, not one was intoxicated, or guilty of profane language. Not long after this time, a sermon was preached in London, before both houses of parliament, the Lord Mayor and Aldermen of London, and the Westminster Assembly of Divines, constituting the most remarkable auditory which the world could then have brought together. In that sermon, the preacher said;—"I have lived in a country where in seven years I never saw a beggar, nor heard an oath, nor looked upon a drunkard." That country was New England. In another place, additional testimony will be presented as to the high tone of morality in the first age of this country.

Mr. Cotton was by no means forgotten in his native country. The times were coming, when "carousing cavaliers were turned to flight in every fight and skirmish," by "praying Puritans," those warriors of "iron grimness, stern as doom." It was about to be ascertained that solid "round-heads" were much too hard for empty "rattle-heads." The Long Parliament had begun to take matters in hand as parliaments had never done before. That persecuting power, which had banished from Britain so many of the choice spirits of the land, was now broken; and many of the wanderers were returning to their homes, while others were earnestly invited to avail themselves of the altered state of affairs. In 1641, a letter was addressed to Mr. Cotton and several other leading colonists, entreating them to return to the mother-country, and to take the part which would naturally fall to them, if there, in remodeling the institutions of the land. This letter was signed by the leading men in that great revolution, including Oliver Cromwell. It was even in contemplation to send over a ship expressly for him.

The next year, Mr. Cotton was invited, with Mr. Hooker and Mr. Davenport, to repair to

England, and partake in the labors of the famous Assembly of Divines at Westminster. Mr. Cotton and Mr. Davenport were at first disposed to comply with the invitation, but were dissuaded by Mr. Hooker. The latter was decidedly opposed to the measure. He probably foresaw, that the overwhelming preponderance of Presbyterian members in that Assembly would probably create great difficulty for any who were so fully committed in conscience and principle to the Congregational Way, as himself and his brethren here. There were in that Assembly, five Congregationalists, commonly distinguished as the "Dissenting Brethren." These, with some help from about as many more of lesser note, kept the whole Assembly at bay for long years of debate and toil. The great body of the members was deeply intent upon establishing a government by Presbyteries, Synods, and Assemblies, over all the churches of England, without any toleration of other sects. They labored in this work with immense vigor, having all the power of the Long Parliament to back them. But do what they would, the invincible "Dissenting Brethren" had the amazing address to embarrass all their attempts. It was long before they could effect any thing, except the preparation of the Catechisms, Confession of Faith, and such doctrinal articles, in which they all agreed. And when at last, with extreme difficulty, the Assembly had completed their complicated model of church-government, and had begun to get a part of the machinery into actual operation, it was too late! All the wheels were broken at once, when Cromwell stamped with his heavy heel, and the Long Parliament vanished.

Of that redoubtable "Five," were Dr. Goodwin and Philip Nye, who knew of old what a perilous debater Mr. Cotton could be. Right glad would they have been, in those "wars of the Lord," to have had the aid of three champions from New England. But these latter were, doubtless, better employed in completing and settling the work in which they were here engaged. Mr. Hooker and Mr. Cotton were then occupied in the preparation of "A Survey of the Sum of Church-Discipline." The first copy of this work was lost at sea by shipwreck on its way to England to be printed. Another copy had a happier passage, and was published at London in 1648. It is in two books; of which the first is by Mr. Hooker, and the other by Mr. Cotton. On the title-page first printed, the whole work is attributed to Mr. Hooker: from which it has happened that Mr. Cotton's share in it has escaped the notice of most of those who have spoken of it. This was a very important treatise in its day; and it was edited and prefaced by Dr. Goodwin. The editor, alluding to the loss of the original copy, makes a remark upon it worth transcribing. "The destiny which hath attended this book, hath visited my thoughts with an apprehension of something like an omen to the cause itself: that after the overwhelming of it with a flood of obloquies, and disadvantages, and misrepresentations, and injurious impressions cast out after it, it might in the time which God alone hath put in his own power, be again emergent." He also compares the cause to seed-corn, which, if it fall to the ground and die, together with some of those who scatter it, shall at last bring forth much fruit. These presages seem to be in latter stages of fulfillment. For, though long depressed, and, in a manner buried, the principles of Congregationalism have never, since the primitive ages, spread so rapidly as of late years.

Most of the ablest treatises which appeared in defence of those principles in the seventeenth century, went from New England. Mr. Cotton did more in this way than any of our divines: but valuable books were prepared by Hooker, Davenport, Stone, Allen, Shepard, Richard Mather, Thompson, Welde, Norton, and others. This was the great controversy of their day. Our fathers studied it with care. There was scarcely a minister of note among them, who did not preach and publish upon it. They were far enough from setting the pattern for that spurious liberality, which is now so much in vogue, and which dreads to have any thing said or done about Congregationalism for fear of making it sectarian.

In the year 1643, all the ministers in the country, to the number of fifty, assembled at Cambridge. "They sat in the college, and had their diet there after the manner of scholars' commons, but somewhat better, yet so ordered as it came not to above sixpence the meal for a person." This frugality is the most remarkable thing recorded of this synod. Mr. Cotton and Mr. Hooker were the moderators. The main business was, to dissuade the Newbury ministers, Thomas Parker and James Noyes, from attempting to introduce the Presbyterian government in their church.

While we are upon synods, we may as well speak of the most important meeting of the kind ever held in New England. It was convened at Cambridge late in 1646, under the auspices of the magistrates. After three sessions, the last of which terminated on the 28th of August, 1648, they presented to the churches and the civil government, the celebrated "Cambridge Platform of Church Government." Having fully discussed the work, the General Court at its next meeting but one "thankfully accepted thereof, and declared their approbation of the said Platform of Discipline, as being, for the substance thereof, what they had hitherto practiced in their churches, and did believe to be according to the Word of God." It thus received in Massachusetts the sanction of law: and indeed was adopted in all the New England colonies, Rhode Island excepted, till the Saybrook Platform was adopted in Connecticut sixty years after. I believe that the articles of faith in very many of our churches, expressly recognize the Cambridge Platform as presenting the principles of ecclesiastical order recognized and practiced by them. And yet if any one were to inquire how many, out of the thousands of members of those churches who have subscribed that declaration, have ever read the instrument referred to, the result would be, perhaps, more curious than gratifying. Less actual inconvenience, however, has resulted from the too general omission of the duty of examining this instrument, than might have been expected. The principles of Congregationalism are so few, simple and intelligible, that the people obtain some general understanding of them without much special effort. Still *it would be far better*, if the people who follow our system would read the book in which it is set forth, together with some of the valuable writings which have recently appeared on the same subject.

But little now remains to be considered, except what relates to the personal character and habits of Mr. Cotton.

In the family, he "ruled well his own house;" as became one who so well "ruled his own spirit." If any thing went amiss, he never corrected it in a passion: but, with great deliberation, began by showing what precept of the Bible had been transgressed or disregarded.

At the devotions of the family, morning and evening, he read a chapter, explaining and applying the contents in a practical manner, but briefly. Before and after the reading, prayers were made, though very short and pertinent. He studied brevity in all: for he held, "that it was a thing inconvenient many ways to be tedious in family duties."

The Sabbath he kept most conscientiously from evening to evening: and it is supposed to be from his example, that the custom prevailed so extensively in New England of "resting according to the commandment" at the going down of Saturday's sun. When that evening arrived, he made a larger exposition at family prayer than at other times. Then the children and servants were thoroughly exercised in the catechism, probably using such as were of his own preparation: one of which, called "Milk for Babes," was used for feeding the minds of the New England children for many years after his death. Another, called "Meat for Strong Men," became their diet at a maturer age, "and nourished them up in the words of faith and of good doctrine." The catechising over, there followed prayer, and the singing of a psalm. Mr. Cotton then withdrew to his study, and its devotions, till the hour of repose.

The next morning, after the customary family worship, he retired to his private communion with God, till he went to the house of God, and its public duties. Returning to his home about noon, he at once secluded himself in his oratory or study, into which there must be no intrusion, except for the purpose of carrying him a very slight repast. At the time for afternoon worship, he came forth again, as one who had been holding converse with God in the mount of prayer. Coming back from the sanctuary, he first sought his retirement, and spent a season in closet prayer. He then prayed with his family; after which each one of the household repeated as much as could be remembered of the sermons of the day. In those days, this was the common practice in all Puritan families. Almost every person was provided with a book for the purpose of taking notes: so that the congregation looked, as we should say, like an assembly of reporters. This repetition of sermons was thoroughly attended to: and happy was the youth who could give the most exact account of *text*, *application*, *doctrine*, *divisions* and *uses*. Almost the only relic of this instructive custom which has come down to our day, is the practice, still preserved in some families, "of bringing home the text." While the good old usage was kept up, the want of Sabbath schools for the religious instruction of the young was not much felt. Or rather, there was a Sabbath school, and that of the best kind, in every family. In Mr. Cotton's household, when the repeating of the sermons was finished, with all the remarks and little explanations and discussions to which that exercise had given occasion, the evening meal was served up. After supper, another psalm was sung. Then the good man, lifting up his eyes and hands, would exclaim;—"Blessed be God in Christ our Saviour!"—and the Sabbath was done. Before retiring to rest, he again, in his study, committed all that he had done to that God whom he "served with a pure conscience."

The sanctification of the Lord's day was a very conspicuous trait of Puritan piety. Good Thomas Shepard, gives as a reason for migrating to this country, that he "saw the Lord departed from England when Mr. Hooker and Mr. Cotton were gone." That excellent man was extremely scrupulous in observing God's holy day. His preparations for the pulpit were commonly finished by two o'clock on Saturday afternoon; in allusion to which, he once used these words;—"God will curse that man's labors, that lumbers up and down in the world all the week, and then upon Saturday in the afternoon goes to his study; when as God knows that time were little enough to pray in and weep in, and get his heart into a frame fit for the approaching Sabbath." This bears rather hard on those ministers who are sometimes described as "Saturday-afternoon-men." Such, if any such there be, may derive instruction from the following extract from a letter of Mr. Cotton's, written to Rev. Nathaniel Rogers in 1630. "Studying for a sermon upon the Sabbath day, so far as it might be any wearisome labor to invention or memory, I covet, when I can, willingly to prevent it: and would rather attend unto the quickening of my heart and affections, in the meditation of what I am to deliver. My reason is, much reading, and invention, and repetition of things, to commit them to memory, is a weariness to the flesh and spirit too; whereas the Sabbath day doth rather invite unto an holy rest. But yet *if God's providence* have straitened my time in the week-days before, *by concurrence of other business not to be avoided*, I doubt not, but the Lord, who allowed the priests to employ their labor in killing their sacrifices on the Sabbath day, will allow us to labor in our callings on the Sabbath, to prepare our sacrifice for the people."

Mr. Cotton was always noted for his hospitality. The stranger and the needy were entertained at his table with a pastoral benignity. It was rare that his house was without a guest. It was a gospel inn. He used to say;—"If a man want an heart for this charity, it is not fit such a man should be ordained a minister." While he lived in England, he was noted for his bounty to distressed ministers, many of whom were deprived by prelatical rigor of the means of subsistence before that rigor fell upon him. Many of the refugees who were driven from their flocks in Germany by the persecution then raging in the Palatinate of the Rhine, found a generous friend in him. Some of them were very eminent divines, who requited his kindness in Latin superlatives, the only coin the poor souls could spare.* To his generous practice there is recorded one of those exceptions which "proves the rule." It shall be given in the words of Mr. Whiting, who is speaking of Mr. Cotton's manner of living at Old Boston in Old England. "His heart and doors were open to receive, (as all that feared God, so) especially godly ministers, which he most courteously entertained, and many other strangers besides. Only one minister, Mr. Hacket by name, which had got into the fellowship of famous Mr. Arthur Hildersham, with many other godly ministers, and being acquainted with their secrets, betrayed them into the prelate's hands: *this* man coming into Boston and meeting with Mr. Cotton, the good man had not the heart to speak to him, nor invite him to his house; which, he said, he never did to any stranger that he knew of before, much less to any minister."

Another instance in which Mr. Cotton showed himself to be one of those who "devise liberal things" occurred in 1651, while he was living in America. There was a little Congregational

* In their accounts of him, they styled him;—"Fautor doctissimus, clarissimus, fidelissimus, plurimumve honorandus."

Church of exiled Puritans at Segetea in Bermuda, of which Mr. Nathaniel White was pastor. Banished by their opposers, this little flock retreated to one of the southern islands, a desolate spot where they suffered severe hardship. When the report reached Mr. Cotton, he exerted himself to procure collections for their relief. Near eight hundred pounds was contributed by some six or eight of the poor churches in the Bay. A fourth part of the sum was gathered by the Boston Church, where there was but one subscription that equaled, and none that exceeded, Mr. Cotton's. The money was laid out in corn and other necessaries, and sent, by the hand of two brethren, in a small vessel hired for the purpose. It arrived at its destination, on the very day when the afflicted exiles had made a personal distribution of their last handful of meal, and had no prospect before them but that of speedily famishing to death. On that self-same day too, their believing pastor had preached upon that most suitable text;—"The Lord is my Shepherd, I shall not want." The admiring exiles could not sufficiently express their gratitude for this timely succor from their New England friends. "For the administration of this service not only supplied the want of the saints; but is abundant also by many thanksgivings to God."

In reviewing what his contemporaries have said of Mr. Cotton, we cannot but be struck with the high repute in which he was held for learning. This was a quality in the absence of which, no minister in the days of the Puritans could command respect. A pious and learned ministry, our fathers considered to be a necessary of life. A Dutch scholar of distinction heard Mr. Cotton preach at Boston in Old England, and declared;—"that never in his life had he seen such a conjunction of learning and plainness as there was in the preaching of this worthy man." It was rare for him to allude to his own acquisitions; but in the confidence of friendship, Mr. Cotton once said;—"That he knew not of any difficult place in all the whole Bible which he had not weighed somewhat unto satisfaction." He had an immense library for those days; and an immense acquaintance with it. But his favorite author was one whose name is not apt to be spoken with commendation by "lips polite." Said Mr. Cotton;—"I have read the fathers, and the schoolmen, and Calvin too: but I find that he that has Calvin has them all." When asked in his later days, why he indulged himself in nocturnal studies more than formerly, he answered with a smile;—"Because I love to sweeten my mouth with a piece of Calvin before I go to sleep." It is needless to ask what were the doctrinal sentiments of a man with such a moral taste as this. It is evident that he held to that Pauline system, which is properly the belief of minds naturally strong, or highly illuminated by the Spirit of grace. No person can be both an intelligent and ardent Calvinist, who has not either a profound and penetrating judgment, capable of grasping truths of the first magnitude; or else a heart intensely excited and irresistibly led by that spiritual influence, which the gospel describes as essential to salvation.

The habits of Mr. Cotton, from youth to age, were those of an indefatigable student. He was an early riser, devoting the morning hours to closer application. In his later years, he abstained from any evening repast; occupying the time appropriated to supper in reading, reflection and prayer. Having a vigorous constitution, his life and labors were happily prolonged by careful diet and regular living. He rarely needed any other doctor for the body. Dryden says :

> "The first physicians by debauch were made;
> Excess began, and sloth sustains the trade."

He was "sparing of sleep, more sparing of words, but most sparing of time." His study was his paradise, which he never willingly left, except to do some good office. Unseasonable visitors, who consumed his precious time, he treated with all gentleness and urbanity: but after such an one had retired, he would say with some regret;—"I had rather have given this man an handful of money, than have been kept thus long out of my study." He kept by him a sand-glass which ran for four hours: this turned over three times, measured his day's work. Of this no small part consisted in fervent prayer: for he held with Luther, that he who has prayed well, has studied well.

In the manner of his preaching, Mr. Cotton was plain and perspicuous. He conscientiously forbore to make any display of his vast learning in the pulpit. He addressed himself to the common people. His chief anxiety was, to be understood. He would often say, though apt to handle the deepest subjects;—"I desire to speak so as to be understood by the meanest capacity." When an iron key would unlock the mystery of godliness better than a golden one, he preferred the cheaper, but more useful metal. The wish of his heart, was to glorify God, rather than to win commendation for himself. At the end of all his manuscript discourses, he ever inserted this, or some similar phrase,—"For thy glory, O God!" In him, the fumes of the "odorous lamp" of science never dimmed the light of his piety.

He commonly bestowed great labor upon his public discourses; though he sometimes preached with very great effect when he had no preparation or warning. Sometimes, as he was going to the pulpit, his text would open to him in a new and striking manner; he would then unfold it by the hour, expressing himself with such steadiness and precision, that the most critical of his hearers would not be aware that they were listening to an unstudied effort.

In vindication of his plain and familiar way of preaching, Mr. Cotton would say;—"If I preach more scholastically, then only the learned, and not the unlearned, can so understand as to profit by me; but if I preach plainly, then both the learned and unlearned will understand me, and so I shall profit all." He viewed the subject just as Martin Luther did, as he is reported to have expressed himself in his table talk. When Dr. Erasmus Albert was to preach before the prince-elector, Luther said to him;—"Let all your preaching be in the most simple and plainest manner: look not to the prince, but to the plain, simple, gross and unlearned people; of which cloth the prince himself is also made. If I, in my preaching, should have regard to Philip Melanchthon, and other learned doctors, then should I work but little goodness. I preach in the simplest sort to the unskillful, and the same giveth content to all. Hebrew, Greek and Latin I spare, till we learned ones come together, as then we make it so curled and finical, that God himself wondereth at us." At another time, the stout reformer exclaimed;—"When preachers come to me, to Melanchthon, to doctor Pommern, &c., then let them show their cunning, how learned they be;—they shall be well put to their trumps. But to sprinkle out Hebrew, Greek and Latin in their public sermons, the same savoreth merely of pride, which agreeth neither with time nor place, nor is it pertinent. In the church, among the congregation, we ought to speak, as we use at home in the house, the plain mother-tongue, which every one understandeth, and is acquainted withal."

Of the happy effect of Mr. Cotton's manner of preaching, we have a very pleasing and instructive example in the autobiography of that worthy old soldier of Jesus Christ, Captain Roger Clap. Having spoken of his admission to the Church in Dorchester, at its formation in 1630, he proceeds with the relation of his subsequent experience in religion. "Jesus Christ being clearly preached, and the way of coming to him by believing was plainly shown forth; yet because many, in their *Relations*, spake of their great terrors and deep sense of their lost condition, and I could not so find, as others did, the *time* when God wrought the work of conversion in my soul, nor in many respects the *manner* thereof; it caused in me much sadness of heart, and doubtings how it was with me, whether the work of grace were ever savingly wrought in my heart or no? How to cast off all hope, to say, and verily to believe that there was no work of grace wrought by God in my heart, this I could not do; yet how to be in some measure assured thereof was my great concern. But hearing Mr. Cotton preach out of the Revelations, that Christ's Church did come out of great tribulation, he had such a passage as this in his sermon;—'*That a small running Stream was much better than a great Land Flood of Water, though the Flood maketh the greatest Noise: so*,' saith he, '*A little constant Stream of godly Sorrow, is better than great Horror*.' God spake to me by it, it was no little support unto me. And God helped me to hang on that text; (and through his grace I will continue so to do,) namely, '*This is a faithful saying, and worthy of all acceptation, that Jesus Christ came into the world to save sinners*.'"* May the words of Mr. Cotton comfort some who read these pages, even as when they came with a blessing to that right old Puritan!

Besides his incessant preaching, and a large correspondence in which he was very usefully

* Memoirs of Capt. Roger Clap. Boston, 1731. Reprinted by David Clapp, Jr. 184 Washington street, 1844, p. 24.

employed as a casuist, being expert in the solving of cases of conscience, he was much engaged in extraordinary labors. In the frequent fast-days appointed by his Church in those troublous times, he would be engaged in prayer and preaching for five and six hours together. He would also keep many whole days of fasting by himself, occupying the time with humiliation of his soul and prayer. He also observed, as occasion prompted, entire days of private thanksgiving for special mercies received.

Of all his more important publications, we have had occasion to speak in the course of this narrative. Most of them were called forth by the controversies which then agitated the Church on the subject of government and discipline. They are remarkable for the mild Christian spirit which pervades them. "None will blame a man," says Thomas Fuller, "for arming his hands with hard and rough gloves, who is to meddle with briers and brambles." But though he had to deal with some of the most thorn-backed and scratching antagonists, they could not provoke him to anger. Though a most tenacious and vigorous maintainer of the truth, he never lost "the meekness and gentleness" which he learned of his divine Master. "It may fairly be said that an amiable spirit in controversy forms one of the most incontrovertible evidences of elevated piety, because it is precisely this point in which so many men of indubitable excellence have failed." Good men have often debated, "as if personal invective, and embittering a style, were God's way of bettering a cause, or battering an opinion." As to the temper in which controversy should be conducted, Mr. Cotton may serve "as a pattern for all answerers to the world's end." Through the spirit in which he replied, he did like Job with the books of his adversaries, "and bound them as a crown to him."

We have alluded to his extensive correspondence. But little of it has escaped the ravages of time. Among others, he maintained a friendly correspondence with archbishop Usher. As a sample of the manner in which he wrote familiarly to his pious friends, an extract is here given from a letter dated the ninth of March, 1631; and addressed to the reverend Nathaniel Rogers, who was afflicted with a very tedious and disheartening malady. "I bless the Lord with you, who supporteth your feeble body to do him service, and meanwhile perfecteth the power of his grace in your weakness. You know who said it, 'Unmortified strength posteth hard to hell, but sanctified weakness creepeth fast to heaven.' Let not your spirit faint, though your body do. Your soul is precious in God's sight; your hairs are numbered; and the number and measure of your fainting fits, and wearisome nights, are weighed and limited by his hand, who hath given you his Lord Jesus Christ, to take upon him your infirmities, and bear your sicknesses."

Among other distinguished correspondents of Mr. Cotton's was one beyond comparison the greatest man of his time. The life of Oliver Cromwell is yet to be written. It has, as yet, been "attempted" only; and that in the most murderous manner. For a considerable period after his death, it would have been regarded as high treason to have presented a true picture of his merits. And when, at last, the expulsion of the Stuarts left historians at liberty to do some justice to Cromwell's character, the age had become too degenerate to understand or appreciate the man. The materials for his history were only such as had been collected by his bitter foes: whose only study was to conceal every thing which could adorn his memory, and parade every thing which could be found or invented to blacken it. The present generation takes its idea of the man, either from Clarendon, who hated his politics; or from Hume, who hated his religion; or from inferior authors, who hated every thing about him. He is commonly regarded as a person of extraordinary talent, but whose talent lay chiefly in the line of canting hypocrisy. His fame, however, is destined to emerge from the clouds which have so long obscured it. Whoever reads, with unprejudiced mind, the recent collection of his letters and speeches, wherein Cromwell speaks for himself in his own way, will feel a revolution in his opinions of the Protector. He possessed the very highest capacity for both military and civil affairs, ranking him among the very first of soldiers and statesmen. To this he added a piety the most profound and unaffected, constantly and naturally pervading all language, whether on the most private or public occasions. He assumed the high station which he so ably filled, in obedience to what he felt to be a divine call, requiring of him what he alone could have effected,—the preservation of the peace, liberty and religion of his distracted country.

In Carlyle's collection we find the first of Cromwell's letters to Mr. Cotton, which was all written with the Protector's own hand. In connection with it, that strange "elucidator" remarks in his own fantastic idiom as follows;—"Reverend John Cotton is a man still held in some remembrance among our New England friends. A painful preacher, oracular of high gospels to New England; who in his day was well seen to be connected with the Supreme Powers of this Universe, the word of him being as a live coal to the hearts of many." Carlyle supposes that Cotton had been writing to Oliver concerning some act of Parliament for propagating the gospel in New England. This is a mistake. The Protector had written to Rev. William Hooke, who was Mr. Davenport's colleague at New Haven; and who, a few years after was one of Oliver's chaplains. In his letter to Mr. Hooke, Oliver had sent loving and respectful salutations to Mr. Cotton. Mr. Hooke, whose wife was near of kin to Cromwell, intimated the message to Mr. Cotton, with the suggestion that a letter from him to the Protector would be taken in good part. Mr. Cotton accordingly wrote a letter of some length, which is preserved in Hutchinson's Collection. It is occupied, after the manner of a solution of a case of conscience, with a cautious vindication of Cromwell's policy, especially in the matters of dosing the Long Parliament with "Pride's purge," and demanding justice upon the head of a perjured and traitorous king. Mr. Cotton, having summed up the considerations belonging to the case in a manner accordant with the views which Cromwell himself appears to have taken of it, goes on to say;—"These things are so clear to mine own apprehension, that I am fully satisfied, that you have all this while fought the Lord's battles, and the Lord hath owned you, and honored himself in you, in all your expeditions; which maketh my poor prayers the more serious, and faithful, and affectionate, (as God helpeth,) in your behalf." This letter is dated the twenty-seventh of May, 1651. Cromwell's reply is dated the second of October following. It owns, as Carlyle says, "Their general relationship as Soldier of the gospel and Priest of the gospel, high brother and humble one; appointed, both of them, to fight for it to the death, each with such weapons as were given him."* Other letters, now lost, passed between them.

In stature, Mr. Cotton was rather low, and slightly inclined to be robust. He had a fair complexion, and ruddy countenance: and his locks, which were naturally brown, in his later life had a snowy whiteness, which, as "a crown of glory" made our patriarch's aspect venerable to behold. There was an inexpressible majesty in his mien, which compelled the respect of all who approached him: and the voice of profaneness was hushed when he was by. The innkeeper at Derby, where Mr. Cotton often visited while he dwelt in England, used to tell his companions that he wished that man were out of his house, for he was not able to swear with him under his roof.

His voice was not strong; but clear and distinct, and heard with ease in the largest assemblies. He delivered himself in the pulpit with much dignity, using a natural and becoming gesture of the right hand. But such a divine power and holy unction attended his grave and

* Oliver Cromwell's Letters and Speeches, Letter CXXV.

earnest manner, that Mr. Wilson said of him;—"Mr. Cotton preaches with such authority, demonstration and life, that methinks, when he preaches out of any prophet or apostle, I hear not him; I hear that very prophet and apostle: yea, I hear the Lord Jesus Christ himself speaking in my heart." O this is the true Christian eloquence, when the lips of the ambassador seem to breathe the very words of the Lord of life and salvation!

He had an almost miraculous evenness of temper. No insult could disturb his self-possession. Such was the meekness and mildness of his disposition, that Mr. Norton used to regard him as the Moses and Melanchthon of the new world. In the words of that good old puritan, Simeon Ashe, "he was a dwarf in regard of humility, but a giant in regard of strength." Though but a lamb in his own cause, like his master, he was a lion in that of God and his church. His gentleness had nothing about it, either nerveless or cowardly. His chief services in behalf of the truth he loved were ever marked by a modest estimation of himself. "The highest flames," says Jeremy Taylor, "are the most tremulous: and so are the most holy and eminently religious persons more full of awfulness, and fear, and modesty, and humility." Mr. Williams, when his adversary, candidly owned the goodness of his heart, and commended his attachment to the truths of the gospel. Mr. Cotton once said to a confidential friend;— "Angry men have an advantage above me: the people dare not set themselves against such men, because they know it will not be borne; but some care not what they say or do about me, because they know I will not be angry with them again."

As a specimen of the manner in which he met abusive treatment, we are told, that he was once followed from the church to his home by a peevish, complaining hearer, who tried to provoke him by telling him, that his preaching had latterly become either very dark, or very flat. To this he mildly answered, "Both, brother, it may be, both: let me have your prayers that it may be otherwise."

On another occasion a very ordinary sort of a man had boasted of his clear insight into the book of Revelation. Mr. Cotton modestly replied;—"Well, I must confess that I want light in those mysteries." Upon this, the man sent him by a servant a pound of candles. The good minister received this piece of impudence with a silent smile; revenging himself only by a christian taciturnity. Mather, relating the circumstance in his magniloquent style, remarks;—"Mr. Cotton would not set the beacon of his great soul on fire, at the landing of such a little cock-boat."

The excellent Mr. Flavel relates an incident of this kind. While Mr. Cotton lived at Boston in old England, he was seen passing along the street, by some gay young fellows, who had been at the tavern, indulging in that, which Solomon says, is a mocker: and is never more so than when it makes mockers of those who use it. One of them says to his companions;—"I will go and put a trick upon old Cotton." Crossing over to the reverend and holy man, he whispered in his ear;—"Cotton, thou art an old fool." That good man, without the slightest irritation, looked mildly at him, and replied;—"I confess I am so: the Lord make both me and thee wiser than we are, even wise unto salvation." Returning abashed to his companions, the wanton insulter told them of this meek reply, which sobered for that time their intemperate mirth, and perhaps first taught them "how awful goodness is."

These examples provoke a sort of impatience, that more of his expressions have not been preserved. We are sure that he daily uttered such instructive dictates of a mind, adorned with unaffected humility, singularly refined from the dross of earthly passions, and mellowed to a sweet maturity of grace by the ripening warmth of close communion with the Lamb of God.

The labors of Mr. Cotton were hastening to a close, by exposure to wet in passing the ferry to Cambridge, where he went to preach to the students. This sermon was from Isaiah 54: 13. "And all of thy children shall be taught of the Lord." Among those who heard it, was Increase Mather, then a young scholar, and in after life married to Mr. Cotton's only surviving daughter. Dr. Mather never forgot the impressions made upon his mind by that discourse. His powers of utterance failed while speaking. He was attacked with inflammation of the lungs, became asthmatic, and was seized by a complicated disease, which he felt as a warning that his end drew nigh.

The next Sabbath he took for his text the last four verses of the second epistle to Timothy, on which epistle he had been expounding in course.

He told his auditory the reason of his taking so many verses at once ;—" Because else," said he, " I shall not live to make an end of this epistle." On the following Sabbath, being the twenty-fifth of November, he delivered his last sermon with much difficulty, on John 1: 14, on the glory of Christ, "from the faith to the sight of which he was hastening." He had the feelings of another of the non-conforming divines, who said ;—" If I must be idle, I had rather be idle under ground, than above ground." He chose rather to *be* dead, than *live* dead : having often expressed a wish that he " might not outlive his work."

This duty done, Mr. Cotton spent one day in his study, in special prayer and preparation for the last great conflict which he was assured was at hand. On leaving that beloved and familiar apartment, he remarked to his consort ;—" I shall go into that room no more ! " He now betook himself to the couch, where he expected " the mercy-stroke of death," the blow that must shatter the last link with which sin or sorrow could fetter his soul. Although his foretastes and promises of heaven chiefly attracted him thitherward, he declared that it greatly contributed to his readiness to depart, when he considered the company of saints, so many of whom he had known and dearly loved, in whose communion he was shortly to mingle.

Magistrates, clergymen, and private Christians in great numbers resorted to his sick-bed, mournfully listening to his dying counsels. Mr. Dunster, at that time President of Harvard College, with many tears besought his blessing, saying; "I know in my heart, they whom *you* bless *shall* be blessed." Shortly before his death, Mr. Cotton sent for the elders of the church, who prayed over him. He exhorted them to feed the flock of which they were overseers, and to watch against those declensions to which he saw that professors of religion were tending. He added;—"I have now, through grace, been more than forty years a servant unto the Lord Jesus Christ, and have ever found him a good master." When his colleague, Mr. Wilson, a man who abounded in love as much as Mr. Cotton did in light, took his last leave, he breathed an ardent wish that God would lift up the light of his countenance upon the dying man; he promptly replied;—"God hath done it already, brother!" He then called for his children to whom he left the covenant of God as their chief portion.

Having settled all his affairs, and taken leave of the world, he begged to be left alone for the little time he had to live, that his soul might be undisturbed in communing with his God. He caused the curtains to be drawn, and exacted a promise of the gentleman who attended him, that the privacy of his chamber should not be interrupted. Then reminding that gentleman, who was a beloved member of his church, of that promise, he gave him this parting benediction;—"The God that made you, and bought you with a great price, redeem your body and soul unto himself!" These were the last words he was heard to utter. After a few speechless hours, he quietly breathed out his spirit into the hands of Him who gave it. This gentle translation of his soul from earth to heaven, took place shortly after eleven o'clock of Thursday morning, the twenty-third of December, 1652, in the sixty-eighth year of his age. On the twenty-eighth of the same month, he was honorably interred by a mourning concourse of the people, among whom he had ministered in holy things for more than nineteen years. He was borne on the shoulders of his brother-ministers to his last sleeping place, in a tomb of brick, in what is called the "Chapel Burying Ground." A deep and sincere mourning was made for him by his afflicted flock, with whom all the scattered churches of New England joined their sorrows; and numerous elegies, according to the taste of the times, recorded the general grief. The lectures in his church during the following winter, preached, as they were by the neighboring clergymen, were but so many funeral discourses. In the first of them, by his old friend and fellow-laborer and fellow-sufferer, Richard Mather of Dorchester, he gave the following counsel to the church;—"Let us pray that God would raise up some Eleazer to succeed this Aaron: but you can hardly expect, that so large a portion of the Spirit of God should dwell in any one, as dwelt in this blessed man." His departure was lamented as a public loss in all the churches of the country. In particular, Mr. Davenport most tenderly bewailed it in a sermon at New Haven, from the words;—"I am distressed for thee, my brother, very pleasant hast thou been unto me."

The south part of Mr. Cotton's dwelling-house was built by Sir Henry Vane, who boarded there with him till Sir Henry returned to England, first giving that addition to Seaborn Cotton. It stood on the lot south of what was lately the estate of Gardner Green, Esq.; and was part of the ground now occupied by the "Tremont Row," nearly opposite to the Savings Bank. That rise of ground long bore the name of "Cotton's Hill." His house was still standing, then the oldest house in Boston, some twenty years ago. The inventory of his estate amounted to one thousand and thirty-four pounds, four shillings. His will provided, that, in certain contingencies, half of his estate should go to Harvard College, and half to support the free school in Boston. Those contingencies never happened: but the provision made for them evinces his deep interest in the important work of education. To the Church he bequeathed a piece of silver plate to be used at the communion table, where at his first coming he had made use of wooden chalices. This reminds us of the lament uttered by one of the writers in the middle ages, who sighs for those days of primitive piety, when the church in her poverty had wooden cups, but golden priests: but now, alas! he cries, we have golden chalices and wooden priests.

The first place of worship in which he here officiated, and which was the first ever erected to God upon this peninsula, stood in what is in these republican days State street, but in those monarchal times was King's Street. It was built in 1632. There are lovers of liturgic pomp, who cannot feel the spirit of devotion unless awakened by columned aisles, and stained windows, and splendid altars, and sacred vestments, and responsive readings, and resounding organs, and choral chants. Such worshipers, as it has been forcibly said, "seem to have no idea of the Supreme Being but as a Grand Master of ceremonies to the whole universe." They would have scorned the adorations of that mud-walled edifice, with its lowly roof of thatch, where, for eight years of sadness, Wilson and Cotton, with their exiled flock, worshiped in spirit and in truth the Father who "seeketh such to worship him." Let that humble structure be commemorated with those wattled temples, in which the first converts to Christianity among our British sires, who dwelt in what was then a land as savage and heathen as was this, before the pilgrims came, sang high praises to the babe that was laid in the manger at Bethlehem.

The second house of worship was built in what is now called Cornhill Square in 1640.

After standing for seventy-one years, it was rebuilt in Cornhill Square in 1712. After the lapse of near a century, the First Church removed, and built the present meeting-house in Chauncy Place. Oh, who that passes by that venerated sanctuary, can refrain from calling to mind that holy and apostolic succession of men of God, from the warm-hearted Wilson to the orthodox and eloquent Foxcroft, who have ministered to that famous Church, and the multitude of its sainted dead? And who that reflects upon the fearful falling away of that assembly from the faith of their fathers, can suppress the lamentation of the prophet;—"How is the gold become dim! how is the most fine gold changed!"

During the nineteen years and more, that Mr. Cotton presided in that Church, one thousand and thirty-four children received the seal of baptism. Of these four hundred and fifty-six were females; and five hundred and thirty-eight were males, being a large excess in favor of the latter. The number of baptisms in each year, exceeded fifty. On this duty of sealing the children of the covenant, and placing Christ's mark upon the lambs of his flock, the teacher laid great stress, and imparted much instruction, some part of which remains in print.

During the same period, there were admitted to the Church, three hundred and six men, and three hundred and forty-three women: in all six hundred and forty-nine, being an average of thirty-four admissions in each year. Seventeen persons had been publicly admonished for different offences; and five of them who could not be reclaimed, were cut off by excommunication. Considering the numbers of the Church, and the strictness of the watch and discipline then maintained, so small a number of ecclesiastical censures argues great purity and blamelessness on the part of the members at large.

Mr. Cotton had three sons and as many daughters; all by his second wife. Seaborn Cotton, his oldest child, graduated at Harvard College in 1651. He was ordained the second minister of Hampton in New Hampshire, in 1660, where he spent his days in great usefulness and honor. He died the nineteenth of April, 1686, aged fifty-two years. He was succeeded by his own son, John Cotton, who also died there at the same age of fifty-two.

The second son of the patriarch of Boston, John Cotton the younger, graduated at Harvard College in 1657. For several years he preached to the Indians at Martha's Vineyard, in their own language. He was ordained at Plymouth in 1669, and labored there in the ministry with great diligence and success for thirty years, both among the whites and Indians. In his fifty-ninth year he removed to Charleston, South Carolina, where he gathered the Congregational Church, which still exists, and is one of the principal churches in that city. He died in less than a year after, on the eighteenth of September, 1669. His son, Roland Cotton, graduated at Harvard in 1685, and was ordained the first minister of Sandwich, Massachusetts, in 1694. He also preached to the Marshpee Indians, of whom, in 1693, two hundred and fourteen were under his care, while five hundred others in the neighborhood of Plymouth were under the care of his father. Roland Cotton died at Sandwich in 1722. He had a brother, Josiah Cotton, who graduated at Harvard in 1698. He was Clerk of Court, Register of Deeds, and Judge of the Common Pleas. He also preached to the Indians, at five different stations, for nearly forty years. He died the nineteenth of August, 1756, aged seventy-five. Three other brothers of Roland and Josiah were ministers. Roland had three sons who were ministers of repute, John Cotton at Newton, Nathaniel Cotton of Bristol, and Ward Cotton of Boylston. Josiah Cotton of Plymouth had a son John, who was the first minister of Halifax.

There have been many other descendants of the Boston minister, who have inherited his name and calling. In him there was a fulfillment of the promise;—"My Spirit that is upon thee, and my words which I have put in thy mouth, shall not depart out of thy mouth, nor out of the mouth of thy seed, nor out of the mouth of thy seed's seed, saith the Lord, from henceforth and forever." It may be said of the posterity of very many of the pious settlers of this "New English Canaan;"—"Their seed shall be known among the Gentiles, and their offspring among the people: all that see them shall acknowledge them, that they are the seed which the Lord hath blessed."

But we must revert to the immediate family of the venerable saint of Boston. His youngest son, Roland, and his oldest daughter, Sarah, died nearly at the same time, at an early age, of the small pox, which raged in Boston in 1649. Sarah died on the twentieth of November. Her last words to her parents were;—"Pray, my dear father, let me now go home." In a few lines of his we find the following language of pious acquiescence in this affecting wish;—

"Go then, sweet Sara, take thy Sabbath rest,
With thy great Lord, and all in heaven, blest."

Roland died nine days after his sister, on which sad occasion, the submissive father again vented his feelings in his antiquated measures.

"Suffer, saith Christ, your little ones,
To come forth, me unto,
For of such ones my kingdom is,
Of grace and glory too.
We do not only *suffer* them,
But *offer* them to thee;
Now, blessed Lord, let us believe,
Accepted that they be."

Of Mr. Cotton's younger daughters, one was married to a respectable merchant by the name of Egginton, but did not long survive the birth of her only child. The child also in a few years followed the mother to the grave. The other daughter of Mr. Cotton became the wife of Increase Mather, D. D., one of the most useful men to Massachusetts whom that "mother of great men" has ever produced. Through Mrs. Mather, her father became the ancestor of several of the most distinguished ministers of the country. His celebrated grandson, Cotton Mather, in our days so grossly slandered and maligned, has noticed an interesting fact in regard to the second, or Old North Church in Boston. The formation of this church, in 1649, appeared to be quite detrimental to the interests of Mr. Cotton; and yet he cheerfully encouraged the undertaking, because it seemed to be required by the interests of religion. Now, of that very church, his son-in-law was pastor above threescore years, and his grandson for forty-four.

Mr. Cotton's widow became the second wife of Rev. Richard Mather of Dorchester, the father of her son-in-law, to whom she thus became a parent by a double affinity. She survived her second husband, with whom she lived in great happiness for many years.

We thus close our account of John Cotton, and those connected with him. That star rose brightly on the older England, and rode through stormy skies. But it sweetly shed its parting rays on the newer England, at its serene and unclouded setting. We close with the following extract from his funeral elegy, by Benjamin

Woodbridge, D. D., which, doubtless, afforded to the philosophic printer, Dr. Franklin, the hint of his famous epitaph upon himself;—

> "A living, breathing Bible; tables where
>   Best covenants at large engraven were;
> Gospel and law in his heart had each its column;
>   His head an index to the sacred volume;
> His very name a title-page; and next
>   His life a commentary on the text.
> O what a monument of glorious worth,
>   When in a new edition he comes forth,
> Without erratas, may we think he'll be
>   In leaves and covers of eternity.

www.ingramcontent.com/pod-product-compliance
Lightning Source LLC
LaVergne TN
LVHW020247110826
845151LV00003B/1041

* 9 7 8 1 4 2 5 5 2 8 7 1 3 *